LONELINESS: A MATTER OF CHOICE

How Our Choices Make Us Lonely

PINGOLIKA BORKATAKI

Clever Fox® PUBLISHING
Chennai • Bangalore

CLEVER FOX PUBLISHING
Chennai, India

Published by CLEVER FOX PUBLISHING 2025

ISBN: 978-93-6707-599-9

CONTENTS

For Maa, Deuta, and my husband.

And for the millions who fight silent battles with loneliness.

INTRODUCTION

"Loneliness and the feeling of being unwanted is the most terrible poverty."

– Mother Teresa

31st August, 1999. It was a hot and humid afternoon in a quiet town in Assam. The road stretched wide and empty, untouched by the stir of a single soul. While everyone else sought refuge indoors, I sat on the veranda, legs curled beneath me, and my eyes fixed on the empty path. Every time I heard the faint crunch of bicycle wheels over gravel, my heart would leap in anticipation. Was it him? The postman? Was this the letter I'd been waiting for?

My father had left for Amritsar to attend a week-long conference just before my seventh birthday, but before he left, he made me a promise. "I might be far away on your birthday," he said. "But you'll have a letter from me as your birthday gift. I promise."

From that moment on, his words became a melody in my mind, playing on loop. I was more excited than I had ever been for any birthday. Back then, the idea of instant phone calls or seeing each other through a screen from miles away felt like something out of a fairy tale. So, for a six-year-old me, the only way to feel my father's presence was through a simple letter. Somehow, that piece of paper felt more powerful than any cake or present. It brought me closer to him, even from thousands of miles away.

Fast forward twenty-seven years, and technology has completely transformed the way we communicate. Today, with a few taps on my phone, I can not only hear my father's voice all the way from India to South Korea, but I can also see the soft wrinkles on his face, the grey strands in his hair, and even the tears that come out when he laughs his heart out. What once seemed unfamiliar and unusual is now a normal part of life. I can appreciate how technology has changed the root of communication and brought us closer, even when we're worlds apart.

But deep down, I still hold on to those simpler days. No matter how sharp the image is on my screen now, that old letter still feels warmer. Sure, it's easy to connect through a video call today, but somehow, it doesn't carry the same weight as a letter that took time, effort, and intention. Even now, I smile when I think about holding his letter for the first time–how I read it over and over, picturing him sitting across from me, adjusting his glasses the way he always did before saying something meaningful.

I couldn't shake the strange feeling that I was more emotionally fulfilled back then, when all I had was my imagination, than I am now, with his face and voice just a tap away. Over the years, something beautiful has been quietly erased: the efforts in relationships. But how is it that swapping effort and anticipation for convenience makes our connections feel emptier and less meaningful? I began writing this book in search of a simple answer to this question. But what I found was far more complex. The lack of emotional depth in our relationships in this digital world leads to more than just disconnection–it leads to loneliness. And I'm not alone in this.

In 2004, Facebook was created with the goal of transforming human relationships and bringing people closer together. Two decades later, from a numerical standpoint, it has succeeded in its mission. Today, Facebook has grown into a trillion-dollar empire, and approximately 5.17 billion people are connected through social media.[1] But do these connections bring people closer? Statistics tell a different story. Today, nearly one in three adults globally admits to experiencing profound loneliness. Loneliness has become an escalating global issue, leading experts to call it a "loneliness epidemic."[2]

Loneliness isn't caused by just one reason or a problem limited to any one culture, age group, or corner of the world. Even in culturally rich and socially connected countries like India, nearly 50% of urban elderly individuals report loneliness due to reduced interaction.[3] According to a report published in 2017 by the Jo Cox Commission, in the United Kingdom, more than 9 million adults report feeling lonely sometimes or always.[4]

If we look at Japan, a nation built on a concept of community and togetherness, social isolation has been a persistent issue. A 2024 survey by the Cabinet Office found that a remarkable 39% of adults feared falling into a state of social isolation.[5] A country like South Korea, which is often recognised for its traditional values that emphasise family ties, social connections, and collective identity, faces its own challenges with loneliness. Despite having the highest levels of digital connectivity worldwide, every year, thousands of South Koreans die quietly and alone, cut off from their family and friends. In 2024, the country invested approximately $327 million over the next five years to combat the issue of "lonely deaths". Seoul Metropolitan Government launched "Seoul Without Loneliness", a city-wide initiative to address loneliness and social isolation. The plan includes a 24*7 helpline ("Goodbye Loneliness 120"), online counselling, and community spaces.[6]

These statistics raise a big question: Why do we still feel lonely in a world where technology has continuously built platforms to bring us closer together? The answer lies in the fact that loneliness isn't just about having people around. What really matters is whether those connections provide the emotional and social depth you need.

In the book "Loneliness: The Experience of Emotional and Social Isolation", sociologist Robert S. Weiss breaks loneliness into two types: Emotional Loneliness and Social Loneliness. Emotional loneliness happens when we feel like no one truly understands us on a personal level. There are times in life when it feels like no one really "gets" us, even if we have many friends or people around. It's when we feel like no one accepts us with all our flaws or values us for who we really are. Instead, it's as if the people around us only appreciate the filtered version we post online. And that's the moment when emotional loneliness sneaks in. On the other hand, social loneliness is the opposite of emotional loneliness. It's the feeling of being disconnected from a larger community or group. Even if you have strong relationships with those closest to you, like your parents, spouse, or a few close friends, a lack of broader belonging can still leave you feeling alone. In this case, the broader connections also need to be genuine and meaningful, not just surface-level interactions.

Loneliness is an inevitable human experience that varies from person to person. What makes one person feel lonely might not affect someone else in the same way. It has always been present in some form, evolving alongside the complexities of human society. After World War II, researchers began to take a closer look at the psychological effects of loneliness, particularly among soldiers, displaced individuals, and those whose lives had been deeply affected by the war.[7] However, loneliness wasn't a major focus of research at the time. It often took a back seat to more prominent topics like depression, grief, child development, and trauma.

Even before 1940, loneliness was rarely discussed because society's structure provided constant social connections.[7] People lived in tight-knit communities, where daily interactions and regular contact with family, work, or social ties helped ward off loneliness. During that time, it was occasionally mentioned in literary or philosophical works. Thinkers like Aristotle in the 4th century and Jean-Jacques Rousseau in the 17th-18th century wrote about the human need for connection, while writers such as Emily Dickinson and Henry David Thoreau in the 19th century explored themes of solitude and isolation.[8]

But today, loneliness has taken centre stage, stealing the spotlight in discussions we never thought we'd have to have. In 2023, Dr. Vivek Murthy, the U.S. Surgeon General, issued a Surgeon General's Advisory titled "Our Epidemic of Loneliness and Isolation". Companies like ElliQ and Panion are working on providing a sense of companionship through technology. The main reason is that what was once a quiet, personal experience has now evolved into a serious concern with both mental and physical health implications.

Studies have found that loneliness increases the likelihood of falling into depression by 33%. Even more alarming, it can raise the risk of dying by suicide by as much as 16 times.[9] Anxiety and depression rates among adults nearly tripled during the COVID-19 pandemic, with loneliness playing a key role in these increases. According to the World Health Organisation, chronic loneliness carries a comparative mortality effect equivalent to smoking 15 cigarettes a day.[10] Loneliness can also drive people toward unhealthy behaviours. Some individuals may resort to overeating, excessive alcohol consumption, or a sedentary lifestyle to cope with their feelings of isolation.

The physical and mental toll of loneliness has been steadily increasing over time. To find a real solution, we need to start by asking why this is happening in the first place. Is it simply our fate? Or something beyond our control? Or are we, in some way, contributing to it ourselves?

It's very easy to blame the digital world for stripping away emotional depth and making both emotional and social loneliness worse. However, viewing loneliness simply as a byproduct of technology oversimplifies a much more complex human experience. Before accepting loneliness as our inevitable fate, this book will encourage you to pause, look in the mirror, and ask yourself: Aren't our choices significantly contributing to the rise of loneliness? No one forces us to choose screens over honest conversations, prioritise comfort over face-to-face connection, or cast judgments that push others away. We are the ones who build these habits that shape the world we live in. Maybe, without realising it, our patterns are quietly building a world of isolation–brick by brick. Maybe our daily choices leave us lonelier than we were ever destined to be. If this is the case, then the solution lies in reexamining how we engage with the world and the choices we make, individually and collectively, to reconnect and rebuild the emotional and social depth that's missing.

Loneliness probably existed long before we could even understand its meaning. When animals feel isolated, they too seek connection, suggesting that loneliness has been part of life before humans started dealing with complex emotions. This book doesn't pretend to offer a cure or to erase loneliness as if it never existed. Instead, it serves as a wake-up call. Each chapter invites you to reflect on our choices, so those choices don't lead us deeper into disconnection, but toward something more human, more intentional, and less lonely.

The first three chapters explore how we've slowly drifted away from genuine connection and empathy, replacing them with a need for validation, constant comparison, and quick judgment. Chapter One explores how choosing digital media provides convenience but only surface-level companionship, quick chats, fleeting highs, and instant gratification at the expense of deeper and more meaningful relationships. Technology isn't the enemy, but it is also not a replacement for genuine human connection. If we don't learn to balance the digital world with real-life interactions, we risk becoming lonelier than ever.

Chapter two highlights how our tendency to judge others by the cars they drive, the clothes they wear, and the homes they buy can make them feel inadequate, forcing them to hide behind carefully curated facades. Judgment rips away the very foundation of empathy, leaving us cold and disconnected. As a result, loneliness becomes almost inevitable in society. Chapter three sheds light on the role of empathy in the growing trend of loneliness. In the name of hustle, we often overlook empathy, forgetting that as it quietly fades, loneliness begins to weave its way into our lives.

The last three chapters focus on how small but powerful shifts in our choices can help us combat loneliness. By choosing to reconnect with nature, embrace solitude, or find a balance between AI, VR, MR, and human interaction, we can create a future that feels less lonely than ever. While the fourth chapter encourages you to explore how spending time in nature can reduce loneliness and restore a sense of belonging, the fifth chapter clarifies that solitude and loneliness are two distinct concepts. Instead of viewing solitude as a weakness, we can use it for self-development, which can become one of the most excellent tools to mitigate the effects of loneliness. The final chapter discusses how the rapid advancements in AI, VR, and other upcoming technologies can impact loneliness. However, if we choose wisely and balance using technology to enhance relationships and ensure it doesn't replace genuine human connection, we can create a world that feels less lonely than it does today.

The loneliness epidemic is deeply rooted in our society, and it's not a problem with a quick fix, nor does it have a one-size-fits-all solution. But by making intentional choices, we can shape a future where loneliness isn't the default setting. This book will have fulfilled its purpose if it inspires even one person to choose authenticity over superficiality, empathy over judgment, solitude over distraction, and nature over relentless scrolling. Sometimes, the smallest shift in perspective is the first step toward meaningful change in the world of loneliness.

With that in mind, let's begin the first chapter and unravel the intricate web of the digital world.

CHOICE 1

DIGITAL ILLUSIONS VS REAL CONNECTION

"We are addicted to our phones because they promise connection, but they deliver isolation."

– Sherry Turkle

It was the last week of February 2018, and the streets of Bangalore were adorned with the striking colours of pink trumpet trees. Their soft colour brought a rare calm to the city's usual rush. Everywhere I looked, people stopped to admire and capture the beauty around them. It felt like the "Silicon Valley of India" had transformed into a stage, with nature putting on a quiet show that everyone was eager to photograph and share.

A month had passed since I relocated to Bangalore for my job. Before moving to the city, I had imagined a life filled with weekend brunches of South Indian food, leisurely walks in the city's breezy parks, hopping between pubs, and making friends who shared my interests. But in the past month, I had hardly found a moment to step outside my apartment or office to appreciate the colourful blooms lining the streets. Every day, I was caught up in the chaos, leaving little room for anything that wasn't tied to my job. The life I had envisioned felt increasingly out of reach as the days passed, buried under the pressure of meetings and deadlines.

I was exhausted. But did my Instagram feed tell the same story about my life?

Not even remotely. My latest Instagram post showed a gorgeous pink road lined with flowers, captioned, "Living my best Bangalore life!" My feed was filled with shades of pink and perfect snapshots. I wanted others to believe I was living an exciting, beautiful, joy-filled life. Everything I posted on social media had one goal: "This is going to look amazing on my feed." At no point did it mean, "This is what I'm truly enjoying."

Am I the only one trying to construct a life on social media that appears more exciting, colourful, and complete than it really is? No, not at all. At some point, we've all done it–crafted a version of ourselves on social media that doesn't quite match the reality. We build this image of happiness, of a life that's perfect for the feed, even if it isn't the full picture.

But why do we all do this? What drives us to present a different version of our lives on social media? Is it the excitement of seeing a few likes from both known and unknown so-called digital friends? Or is it the rush of getting that illusory sense of validation that makes us feel noticed, even for just a moment? Whatever the reason, the consequences are far more dangerous than any temporary satisfaction we get from it.

The circle of pretending begins innocently with a photo that's a little too polished or a caption that's almost too flawless, creating an image of who we wish to be. At first, it feels harmless–nothing more than a simple shift, fueled by the hope that maybe some magic will spill from social media and bring the connections our hearts wish for. And then, when the likes start pouring in and comments from friends pop up, we feel like the centre of attention, even if it's just for a moment.

Before we know it, a quick dopamine hit turns into something more profound: a pattern of performance. Over time, we slowly start to deceive ourselves with every highlight, story, reel, and update. We gloss over every struggle and edit out the raw, unpolished parts of our lives. In the hustle of the crowd, it's easy to convince ourselves we're genuinely connected, even when all we're doing is pretending. But in the quiet moments–when there's no filter, no caption, and no audience–it becomes much harder to believe we're truly living our best life. The gap between the person the world sees and the one who stares back at us in the mirror raises unsettling questions: "Does anyone really understand me?" or "Am I alone in this world?"

Back in 1957, social psychologist Leon Festinger introduced a concept called Cognitive Dissonance that explains much of human behaviour today. In his book, he described the inner conflict we all experience when there is a difference between the version of ourselves we project to the world and the version we keep hidden. Festinger explained that when this dissonance surfaces, our minds scramble to resolve it. We either change our behaviour or come up with reasons to justify the difference–anything to calm that uneasy feeling.[1]

In the context of portraying "Living the best life" on social media, cognitive dissonance has become a daily struggle for many of us.

For instance, imagine you are someone who regularly posts about self-love, confidence, and positivity. Your photos are vibrant, your captions uplifting. To anyone scrolling by, it looks like you've got it all figured out–strong, unshakable, completely at ease in your skin.

But behind the screen, after every post, you overthink, constantly checking to see how many likes you've received and how many comments people have left. You question your appearance, wondering if you look good enough, if you're interesting enough. You crave validation- not just online, but in real life, too. When someone else's post pops up, a success story, a picture-perfect relationship, a new milestone, you can't help but feel that sting of comparison.

In times like these, the life you show on social media can feel miles apart from the one you're actually living. That's when cognitive dissonance begins to set in. It is a quiet tension between how things look and how they really feel. Your mind tries to resolve the conflict, coming up with reasons to explain the mismatch between the polished version you present and the messier truth underneath.

Situations may differ from person to person, but one thing remains common: whenever posting happiness on social media starts to feel like pretending, we all instinctively reach for a justification. At first, we tell ourselves that the likes, the comments, the digital approval will be enough, that they'll fill the gap. And when that reassurance falls short, another excuse quickly takes its place: "This is just how social media works. Everyone does it. No one shows their full, messy truth, so why should I?"

But if we're being honest, really honest, can we ask ourselves this once: do those justifications ever truly calm the discomfort, or do they simply keep us trapped in the performance?

When the discomfort is small, these judgments provide temporary distractions, but they never truly address the emptiness we feel because of the internal struggle. Pretending and justifying the pretence doesn't just lead to exhaustion, it isolates us. No matter how many likes, comments, or followers we accumulate, if those interactions are with an image we've carefully crafted and not the real us, it doesn't really count.

If we try to look into the cause of our need to curate our lives so meticulously, it all comes down to validation. The term "craving for validation" has gained popularity recently in conversations about self-esteem, social media, and mental health, but the desire to be seen, admired and accepted is nothing new for human beings. Centuries ago, kings and nobles weren't posting selfies, but they had their own ways of proving their worth. They hosted lavish banquets filled with exotic foods, extravagant table settings, and grand entertainment–musicians, jesters, dancers–just to impress their guests. It was their way of saying, "Look how powerful and wealthy I am". Before filters and Photoshop, rulers commissioned massive portraits and statues of themselves, carefully crafted to exaggerate their looks and achievements. Kings tried to look taller, more powerful, more grand, because appearance shaped authority. These images were displayed in palaces and important buildings, serving as constant reminders of their greatness.[2]

Even just a decade ago, before the rise of social media, people would invite friends and family over to watch the entire wedding video or flip through wedding albums–sometimes more than once. It wasn't always about reliving the day; it was sometimes about hearing people say, "Wow, your wedding was amazing!" Although the psychology of validation remains in our DNA, the biggest difference between then and now is speed and scale. In the past, a king had to wait weeks for news of his victory to spread. The need for approval was largely limited to a small circle of close friends, family, or colleagues. Validation required effort, and when you got that validation, it only lasted for a short time. But today? Validation is instant and always just a click away. It has become magnified, widespread, and ironically more impersonal.

The real danger begins when we start relying on these digital pats on the back to feel worthy while ignoring the messier, more vulnerable parts of ourselves–the parts that truly make us who we are. We lose sight of the fact that when our sense of worth is built on external approval, it becomes fragile, constantly at the mercy of algorithms, trends, and the attention of others.

Today, validation is no longer just an emotional need. Social media has transformed it into a career necessity for approximately 200 million people worldwide who are on the content creation journey.[3] Being an influencer has become the go-to career track for almost every young person chasing the spotlight. Influencers curate their lives in ways that appeal to followers rather than staying true to their genuine experiences and values. The topics they cover are tailored to what will get them featured on the viral page. When it comes to their emotions, "feeling blessed" has never been more strategically timed. It's less about living real moments and more about curating an idealised life that's always filled with brunches, sunsets, and perfect smiles.

Many would argue that being a social media influencer is just like any other job. After all, it's a way to make a living–one that requires creativity, business acumen and technical skills. They spend time to understand their audience, optimise their profiles and stay on top of trends, much like any professional focusing on advancing their career. They use social media as a tool to build their brand, cultivate a community, and thrive in a digital world.

Yes, it is true. But there's a darker side to this profession. With every post, every reel, every video, the obsession with staying relevant can feel like an emotional treadmill. It often feels like a constant race to keep up appearances. You're always chasing the next like, comment, or share. The need for validation runs deep in this space, more than most are willing to admit, feeding a cycle where self-worth starts to hinge on approval from others.

When the search for validation becomes the priority, it's easy to forget what truly matters–the deeper connections, the authenticity, and the real sense of self-worth that can't be measured in digital interactions. When I left my IT job to pursue content creation, driven by my passion for mental health awareness, I threw myself into the world of social media. I created accounts on every platform, following the golden rule preached by social media experts–ticking off each "must-do" item along the way.

– 5–10 Instagram Stories a day to stay on top – *check*!

- Post 1–3 times daily for those sweet engagement spikes– *check again*!
- 3–7 posts per week to keep the crowd interested–*check that too.*

The list just kept going, and I was all in without question. The formula seemed simple: the more I interacted with social media, the more engagement I received. But no one tells me that to create social media content, I must live in it. I don't just share content; I become part of the never-ending cycle where posting, scrolling, and engaging are all seamlessly blended into my daily life.

I remember those days, waking up and immediately reaching for my phone, scrolling through likes, comments, and followers. I became obsessed with the validation metrics, the constant chase for approval that defined my worth. Despite creating content aimed at promoting mental health awareness, my own mental health began to crumble. I lost touch with my friends and found myself getting irritated over the smallest things. Breakfast, lunch and dinner became less about connection and more about curating moments for social media. I started saying things just because they were trendy, even putting out messages I knew were irrelevant–all in the name of gaining reach. Every time, cognitive dissonance kicked in with the thought, "Is this really what I started for?" I would justify it by telling myself, "Every famous influencer does it. I need to do it too if I want to grow my brand."

I gained 5,000 followers in a month, but in the process, I felt an overwhelming loneliness. This loneliness wasn't because I lacked digital connections. It was because I had become disconnected from my authentic self and distanced from the relationships that truly mattered. The time I used to spend with my husband and my parents grew shorter and more infrequent. This is the harsh truth about glamorous social media: Before we even realise it, we become trapped in a relentless game of validation, leaving us feeling more isolated than ever.

Validation also transforms the way we capture and experience moments. Photographer Berenice Abbott once said, "The photograph is a way to capture the most fleeting moments, the essence of something that is often unspoken." Her words speak to the soul of photography as an art form, a way of holding onto the intangible beauty of life.[4] But today, if I were to ask you, "Are you taking photos to capture the essence of a present moment?" the answer would often be no. Today, photographing has become less about capturing life's fragments and more about how others will judge, measure, and evaluate it.

Back then, the photo albums, now treasured as vintage keepsakes, used to be so much more than just collections of pictures. Those were little time capsules, with each page holding a treasure chest of memories. Even the black-and-white photos, worn with time, seemed to capture moments frozen in a way that felt more tangible, more real. When we opened any old album, we didn't just see images; we felt the nostalgia rush in like the pages were bringing those moments back to life. The memories attached to them, like the laughter, the smells, the sounds, would fill your heart. It brought a smile to our faces, a sense of warmth, and a connection to a past that felt like another time.

But today, photos have become part of the endless scroll of social media feeds. It's so easy–instant access to memories, right there at your fingertips, always ready to relive with a tap. But do they still spark the same joy they once did? Haven't our moments of capturing photos slowly turned into a metric for measuring our happiness through likes and comments? Take the photo of the pink tree I snapped–it should have made me smile every time I saw it. Right? But the moment I posted it, instead of reliving that joy, it triggered a full-blown anxiety marathon. Every passing minute, I found myself back on my phone, compulsively checking how many views it had or whether anyone had commented.

But what if our photos received zero likes? What if no one engaged with it at all?

Honestly, nothing would happen. Unless your livelihood depends on it, most of it doesn't matter as much as you think. Psychologists Thomas Gilovich and Kenneth Savitsky introduced the term "spotlight effect" in their research, highlighting how people tend to overestimate how much others notice or judge their appearance, behaviour, or mistakes.[5] But the truth is, most people are too busy dealing with their own thoughts, worries, and insecurities to really notice what we're doing.

But the cost of prioritising this validation is more significant than we think, as it distracts us from experiencing the authentic moments in our lives and takes us to a feeling of emptiness. In the loop of validation and pretending on social media, we willingly shape our lives to fit in a system that is designed to keep us hooked but not truly emotionally fulfilled. So the real question is: **Are we still willing to overlook the moments that truly**

matter? Our choice will ultimately determine whether we can ease the loneliness we feel.

Convenience and Comparison: The Reality of Digital Friendships

"People are lonely because they build walls instead of bridges."

– Joseph F. Newton

In the mid-20th century, psychologist Abraham Maslow positioned belongingness and love just after our most basic needs, such as food and safety, in his well-known psychological theory "Hierarchy of Needs".[6] He recognised that once our survival is ensured, the next driving force for humans is the need to form relationships and social connections. If you pause to think about it today, this still rings true. The happiest, most fulfilled people in your circle aren't necessarily the ones with the most wealth or status, but those who share deep, meaningful connections with others, who feel anchored by a true sense of belonging. In other words, the need to belong and to feel understood isn't a luxury; it's a fundamental part of our human nature.

While the desire to belong is essential, technology is evolving how we seek connection. We enter social media with one agenda: to feel connected. But somewhere along the way, the purpose blurs. In following the script–scroll, engage, and repeat–we forget that each click pulls us further into an endless loop of digital interaction. It's a loop that promises an authentic connection but delivers only a convenient digital friendship.

Today, we have more digital friends than real ones, and that's because online connections provide an easy way to engage without the need to leave your space or invest in physical effort. On social media, I know exactly what my online friends are up to, what they're eating, and where they're travelling. Keeping in touch now just means liking a photo, leaving a comment, or sending a quick DM like "What's up?" or "Your life looks amazing." They might reply with just a word or two, and before you know it, the conversation ends with a quick, "We'll meet up soon". Nowadays, small talk comes easily, but deep conversations are few and far between. If you asked me when I last had a deep conversation with my best friend about life, dreams, or what truly matters, I wouldn't have an answer.

These days, I see dinner tables occupied by people sitting together, yet each one is absorbed in their phone, scrolling or taking pictures meant for social media, all while missing the chance to actually live in the moment. The very platform designed to connect us often leaves us worlds apart. We're physically present, but are we emotionally there too?

While real connection happens over a cup of coffee, where we sit side by side, talking and listening for hours, digital friendships often unfold through liking posts and sharing memes. This pattern of engaging in superficial interactions gives us an illusion of connection, but in the end, it leaves us feeling empty and unfulfilled. Psychologists refer to this pattern as "social snacking".[7]

Think of social snacking like grabbing a samosa when you're hungry–it might satisfy your hunger briefly but leave you feeling empty until you have a nourishing meal like Daal Chawal or Biryani. The same goes for our emotional well-being. Trust, empathy, vulnerability, patience, and unconditional support are the daal chawal for connection. They're the soul-filling elements that nourish real relationships, leaving us feeling genuinely seen and fulfilled.

But, just like any junk food, digital connections are highly addictive because they are quick and effortless. They let us maintain connections without the emotional risk of vulnerability, making it a tempting shortcut to social engagement. But in the end, they don't nourish us in the way that real and meaningful connections do.

The risk of social snacking arises mainly when we use it as a substitute for genuine engagement. Social snacking might be our first stop, giving us quick bursts of dopamine, but in our most vulnerable or happiest moments, we need more than online phrases. When our hearts break, a notification won't comfort us. A DM can't replace a shoulder to lean on. In our most vulnerable moments, we don't need digital friends–we need real presence. A friend sitting across from us, saying nothing yet somehow saying everything.

Imagine you finally bought your dream car. Your first instinct? You snap a picture, write a caption, and post it online. Within minutes, the likes and comments start flooding in–"Congrats!", "So happy for you!", "You deserve it!" It feels good, doesn't it? But after a while, when the screen goes dark, you realise that something is missing. That something is the warmth of real, human presence. Now, imagine this instead: The day you buy your dream car, you're not alone. Your friends and family gather around, laughing, telling stories, just enjoying being together. Can this moment, filled with genuine connection and joy, bring the same energy as the virtual celebration we seek on social media? The answer will determine whether digital friendships are just a convenient form of connection or a true source of companionship.

The more we replace the organic moments of our daily lives with superficial ones, the more we begin to feel invisible, like we're not really seen or heard. It's no coincidence that Generation Z (born between 1997 and 2012) and Millennials (born between 1981 and 1996), the two most digitally immersed generations, report the highest levels of loneliness.[8] Instead of turning to people physically around them, many in these generations rely on online interactions–DMs, likes, and comments–to feel connected. And yet, that connection feels hollow.

Their experience of loneliness isn't just about being physically alone, but about being lost in the digital maze, where surface-level interactions replace real, deep connections. While offering the illusion of connection, digital friendships also come with the constant undercurrent of comparison. Just like validation, comparison isn't new to us; it's just been supercharged by technology.

Back then, comparison had its limits. In school, we might have measured ourselves against the classmate who always got straight A's. At work, we might have sized up our progress next to the colleague who landed a big promotion. But once we left the classroom or office, we could take a break from it. Social media changed that. Now, comparison follows us everywhere, 24/7, fueled by algorithms designed with one goal: to keep us scrolling. We wake up and check our feeds, instantly reminded of someone else's seemingly perfect vacation, toned body, or big career win. Even our happiest moments can feel overshadowed by someone else's highlight reel.

Digital friendship, which was once meant to be a space for genuine connection, can now inadvertently become a platform for proving, "I'm enjoying the moment as well". Unlike real-world friendships, digital friendships often show only highlight reels, vacation photos, milestones, achievements, and carefully curated snapshots, leaving out the messy, vulnerable parts of life. We begin to believe that everyone else is living a life full of joy and adventure, while our own experiences feel unfulfilling. This creates a negative self-image, slowly chipping away at our self-worth and eroding our confidence. We start thinking we should be as interesting, successful, and happy as those we see online. As a result, instead of celebrating the beauty of friendship, we begin to mimic the lifestyles portrayed on social media.

But should every moment be followed by the thought, "I should do this too, or I'll be left behind?" No, right? Just because someone posts about making traditional laddoos during Diwali doesn't mean you need to replicate the same to feel included. If someone shares reels of their Pinterest-worthy home decorations, it doesn't mean you should feel pressured to follow the same. Digital friendship can spark growth and give companionship, but it requires a lot of self-awareness. We need to recognise that not every aspect of life needs to be compared. It's perfectly okay if your comfort is found in a home-cooked meal rather than an overpriced dish in a fancy restaurant. It's absolutely fine if your job is a 9-to-5, and your best friend is a travel blogger. It's okay if, during winter break, you're not jetting off to an exotic hill station covered in snow.

Over the years, the texture of relationships has changed, and in the coming years, it may change even more. While this evolution is a natural part of how we adapt to new ways of communicating, social interaction shouldn't become a performance. Instead, it should be a genuine exchange that fosters true connection, helping to reduce feelings of loneliness. Before it's too late, we need to put down our phones and return to where we left off–before filters replaced authenticity, before followers became a measure of worth, before we started mistaking digital friendship for real friendships.

But the choice is ours: **Are we ready to choose conversations over comments, and real-life friendships over digital friendships?** Because the moments that truly matter aren't the ones we display –they're the ones we fully live.

Talk to the Camera: The Only Interaction for Miles

"Digital platforms provide an illusion of closeness but may amplify loneliness by keeping real, face-to-face interactions at bay."

– Researchers at the University of Pennsylvania

"Hey guys, welcome back to my channel."

This familiar line invites viewers into the vibrant world of vlogging. When Adam Kontras uploaded the first vlog in 2000, documenting his cross-country journey, no one could have imagined that this simple act of sharing would evolve into a multibillion-dollar industry.[9] Today, with smartphones in our pockets and editing apps at our fingertips, vlogging has become a democratised art form. Millions of vloggers, from celebrities to commoners, are consistently creating high-quality content with strong branding. It has evolved into a global phenomenon, with creators building massive followings and turning their channels into thriving businesses. Revenue streams like YouTube AdSense, affiliate marketing, and exclusive content platforms (Patreon, memberships) are significantly boosting their earnings. In India, vloggers with 100,000 to 500,000 subscribers can potentially earn anywhere from ₹50,000 to ₹5,00,000 per month.[10] Those who diversify their income sources–through sponsorships, merchandise, and premium content–can achieve even higher earnings.

Vlogging has gained tremendous popularity in a very short span of time because it taps into the fundamental human need for connection by creating a space where we can feel like we're part of someone else's life. Whether it's waking up with them, watching them cook breakfast, or tagging along on their latest adventure, vloggers invite us into their personal worlds. They share their lives in a way that feels intimate, and by addressing their viewers as "family," they foster a sense of belonging that many crave.

Psychologists call this phenomenon "Parasocial Relationships"– one-sided bonds where viewers develop genuine attachments to vloggers despite never having met them. The concept dates back to the work of Horton and Wohl (1956), where they introduced the term "parasocial interaction" to describe the illusion of a personal connection with media personalities.[11] But in today's digital world, this dynamic has expanded far beyond celebrities. Anyone through YouTube channels, TikTok, or Instagram stories can become the centre of someone else's emotional connection.

Looking at the brighter side, I'd say parasocial relationships can serve as a lifeline. It offers a sense of belonging when physical company is hard to find. When you watch families share dinners, celebrate little victories, or couples navigate the rollercoaster of life, you feel an undeniable sense of comfort. Apart from personal vlogs, travel vlogs can take us to places we have only dreamed about. They show us sunsets over oceans we wish to witness and streets we hope to explore. For a little while, we are not stuck in our living rooms; we are there, seeing the world through someone else's lens. And it feels good. It feels comforting.

But here's the twist: it's all a performance. No matter how much we care, the other person doesn't even know we exist. In their world, we are nothing more than spectators, and in ours, they are distant figures. We build connections in our minds, but they might never see the words or feelings we send their way. It's a relationship with a barrier, one where we invest so much but receive nothing in return except the illusion of connection.

The real issue arises when the comfort of vlogging becomes a crutch, a way to escape from the messiness of our own lives. When we sit in our own homes, watching strangers share their daily routines, their laughter, their struggles, yet we overlook the voices of those sitting right beside us. When we celebrate the milestones of vloggers we've never met, but forget to check in on the people who genuinely matter. When our own experiences start to feel dull in comparison, and instead of living fully, we settle for observing. And in that slow, imperceptible shift, loneliness creeps in–not as an obvious void, but as a quiet absence of true connection.

Whether you're the one watching from the comfort of your bedroom or the one behind the camera who is curating the perfect moment for their audience, both sides of this digital coin can feel strangely isolating. Imagine a travel vlogger standing before the vast horizon, speaking to a screen for hours, narrating the beauty of a place they longed to visit. They capture every sunrise, every mountain peak, every moment they think someone out there would want to see. But what happens when they pause the camera? When they lower it, and the beauty around them is left untouched by the lens? How many travel vloggers, standing before a breathtaking sunset, can truly enjoy the view without the constant reminder that the lens is watching, without the thought that they are performing for others? How many of them wish, just for a moment, to experience the world not through a camera but as an actual human being, connecting with the people around them without the pressure of being constantly "on"?

Now, imagine a vlogger who puts their heart and soul into every video, showing both the good times and struggles they go through. But what happens when they turn off the camera and step away? Will those online connections still feel as comforting when the screen is off? How does it feel when the vlogger's voice, once so resonant and connected to the virtual crowd, now echoes unheard in the stillness of the room? Doesn't it seem strange that a life shared with thousands, even millions, could feel so distant and detached in the absence of a camera? Isn't it a lonely paradox–an illusion of connection?

The connections we make through a screen can never truly fill the void that exists when the camera turns off.

Today, the vlogging industry is expanding at an unprecedented rate, with an increasing number of youth eager to step into the spotlight. But what role does vlogging play in the loneliness epidemic? While vlogging has become a massive success, we can't ignore the fact that the urge to document every single moment of our lives often pulls us away from truly living those moments. This phenomenon is often referred to as "performative living," where the act of recording overshadows the authentic enjoyment of an experience.[12]

In performative living, the line between online and offline life becomes increasingly blurred. Instead of fully immersing ourselves in the moment, we find ourselves consumed by how it will appear on screen, how it will sound to our audience, or how it will be received in the relentless cycle of content creation. From morning coffee to life's biggest moments, everything feels like something to post. Just living isn't enough anymore; it has to be shared and seen. The camera is always open, not just for memories, but to document even our quietest thoughts and most personal experiences.

Loneliness is a problem that can only be resolved by prioritising authenticity and genuine relationships over appearances and validation, not by looking into someone else's life or constantly creating content about our own. While vlogging can be entertaining and sometimes comforting, it cannot replace the deep, authentic connections that are essential for overcoming loneliness.

Now, it's our turn to choose: **Will we focus on nurturing the connections right beside us, or will we be drawn into the glittering world of vlogging?** Every choice we make has the power to cross that thin line, from entertainment to loneliness.

Confessions of a Podcast

"We are drowning in information but starved for wisdom."

– John Naisbitt

My favourite part of the day growing up was always the evening chai with my mother. It was a time of endless stories. I would ask her about her journey– how she built an educational institution from the ground up, what the world felt like back then, how tough it must have been for a woman back then to chase her dreams and make them real. Every time she answered, a sense of awe and admiration would grow inside me. I wasn't just looking at her as my mother, I was looking at her as a woman whose strength I'd one day need to find in myself. Those conversations weren't rehearsed or scripted; they were raw, unfiltered exchanges between a mother and daughter, flowing as naturally as the warmth of the tea we shared.

Fast-forward to today, and this whole scenario–two people sitting across each other, sipping coffee or tea, swapping life experiences and what they've learned along the way –feels oddly familiar. We call it a "podcast" now. The only difference? When my mother told her stories, I was completely there, sensing the feelings behind her words. On the other hand, podcasts attempt to offer that same wisdom from others' lives but through a screen or a pair of headphones.

It's fascinating how conversations have found a new home in podcasts, allowing us to connect with voices and stories from around the world. The term "podcast" was first coined by British journalist Ben Hammersley in a 2004 *Guardian* article, blending "iPod" (Apple's popular music player) with "broadcast." However, the roots of podcasting trace back further to Adam Curry, often referred to as the "podfather".[13] Curry played a pivotal role in bringing podcasts to life when he developed iPodder in 2004–a program that allowed users to download audio files directly to their iPods, laying the groundwork for the podcasting revolution we know today.[14]

Podcasts make it possible to absorb knowledge and entertain ourselves without ever slowing down. Whether driving through traffic, running on a treadmill, or folding laundry, you can tune in and experience stories, ideas, and insights from anyone. It's a seamless way to keep learning, laughing, and reflecting, all while keeping up with the demands of daily life. But it doesn't stop there. Listeners connect over common interests, discuss the episodes online, and build bonds with like-minded individuals.

Today, from actors to authors, business people to influencers, everyone seems to have a mic in hand and a podcast on air. Podcast is a multi-billion-dollar industry with millions of shows covering every imaginable topic. In 2023, the global podcasting market was valued at $23.63 billion. With a forecasted annual growth rate of 27.6% from 2023 to 2030, experts predict the industry will soar to an impressive $131.13 billion, transforming the way we consume stories, news, and ideas. The number of podcast listeners worldwide also continues to rise, with over 546.7 million listeners in 2024. This number is expected to surpass 600 million by 2026.[15]

But my question remains the same: Are podcasts really giving us valuable wisdom, or are they gradually taking us away from the real human interaction we crave?

Podcasts are no exception to the trend where increased digital stimulation can often lead to a sense of disconnection. Podcasts are undeniably great, until they become an addiction. The signs of unhealthy podcast consumption can be subtle at first. What seems like a harmless habit can gradually turn into an escape mechanism that disconnects us from reality. For instance, if someone constantly plugs in their headphones to avoid conversations or responsibilities, it might indicate they're using podcasts as a distraction rather than a tool for growth. Feeling anxious or restless when not listening to a podcast suggests dependence, much like any other form of digital consumption. Prioritising podcasts over real-life relationships can slowly erode meaningful connections.

It's easy to get caught up in the voices of podcast hosts and guests, feeling as though we are part of a lively conversation with friends. We laugh at their jokes, agree with their insights, and even share in their emotional experiences. But despite these feelings of closeness, the reality is that the hosts and guests have no knowledge of our existence. This can foster a false sense of belonging, where the comfort of passive listening takes precedence over actively seeking social interactions in our own lives.[16]

When everyone has the ability to start a podcast, a crucial question arises: credibility. Are we truly receiving accurate information? Many of us engage with podcasts thinking we're being productive, but we often don't realise when that productive listening turns into consumption of misleading or shallow content. As we plug in endlessly, soaking up wisdom from various hosts without questioning its validity, we risk missing out on the knowledge that is actually true. Not every voice we hear is insightful–some are simply adding to the noise, capitalising on the popularity of podcasts.

Ultimately, as with everything in life, balance is the key. Being mindful of our consumption ensures that we enjoy the benefits of podcasts without letting them take over our daily lives. Yes, podcasts can offer us companionship during moments of isolation, and yes, they can fill the silence with knowledge. But let us not be fooled–their voices cannot hug us when we're broken, they cannot laugh with us in joy, and they cannot share those raw, unscripted moments that only a real human can offer.

Everything depends on our choice: **Will we seek balance, or will we choose the comfort of getting lost in curated voices?**

Is the Digital World Truly All Bad?

"The key to digital well-being is not abstention, but mindful engagement."

– Adam Alter

There's no doubt that today's hyperconnected world has completely revolutionised the way we work, communicate, think, and acquire information. For starters, it allows us to reach thousands of people 24/7, explore diverse career options innovatively, learn about different cultures, and gain exposure to many ideas and perspectives. Online communities give a sense of belonging to people with shared interests or experiences, even when they are thousands of kilometres apart. Influencers shape trends and drive conversations; activists use social media to challenge stigmas and inspire social change through stories. Today, you have the power to shape your financial destiny. Your online presence serves as your billboard, your resume, your first impression, all rolled into one. Whether you are a writer, artist, or just someone with a story to tell, social media gives you the platform to achieve fame and recognition. The content creation market has opened up unprecedented opportunities, allowing us to earn money in ways that were unimaginable a few years back. Today, a 17-year-old teenager may earn more from content creation without a degree than a graduate from IIT or IIM.[17]

So, yes, the digital world isn't all that bad after all. But we can't ignore the irony that countless people feel lonelier than ever because of the same digital world. Whether it's through social media, vlogging, or podcasts, our deliberate choices to stay connected to the world through digital media have come at a cost. Each time we glance at our screens during a conversation, we unintentionally send a quiet message to the people we love: "You're here, but something out there feels more important." Simply having a device within reach subtly reminds us of the vast, constant social network to which we are connected.[18] It's a form of mental tug-of-war – our attention is perpetually drawn toward the distant digital world, leaving the people who should have our complete attention.

It's an irony of our generation. Technology has indeed made "connecting" just a click away, yet we tend to disregard the reality that nothing can truly replace the depth and warmth of face-to-face interactions. This doesn't happen because the digital world is inherently harmful. It happens because we fail to set it aside when real and meaningful connections are right in front of us. And it all starts with a quick glance at our phones during a conversation, thinking it will be just a momentary distraction. But then, another glance, then a third. Each time, we promise ourselves it will be just for a second, a quick check to ease our minds. Yet, before we know it, we find ourselves hours deep in a scroll, helplessly lost in an endless stream of content, completely unaware of how far we've drifted from the world and the people around us.

At the heart of this loop is the social media algorithm - the invisible architects of our digital lives, which is working behind the scenes to analyse our every interaction, what we like, comment on, or share. These algorithms track patterns in our behaviour and use that data to predict what we might want to see next. It's kind of a personalised "filter bubbles" that limit our exposure to diverse perspectives, potentially leading to echo chambers and polarisation.[19]

For instance, if you watch a video of a cute cat doing something hilarious, the algorithm logs that, understands your interest, and feeds you more content of a similar nature. If you interact with influencers who post their perfect lives, then you are shown that type of content is what you like, and before you know it, your feed is full of perfectly curated glimpses into other people's lives.

We're all hooked on this algorithm because our brains are wired to seek new information, keeping us engaged as we hope the next post will be even more interesting than the last. This behaviour is primarily driven by dopamine, the brain's "reward" neurotransmitter. Every time we encounter something new or unexpected, our brain releases a burst of dopamine. This creates a powerful feeling of reward and pleasure, like a mini celebration in your brain. This is why you feel a little rushed when you see a new notification, and you feel oddly compelled to check your phone constantly.[20]

Algorithms are designed with only one purpose: to keep your eyes glued to the screen, understand your habits and vulnerabilities, and keep you coming back for more. So, instead of falling into the trap of endless scrolling, we can take control by setting intentional limits on screen time and prioritising real-world connections. Through a delicate balance between the digital and real worlds, we can unlock unlimited possibilities that once seemed unimaginable just a few decades ago.

The first step toward setting boundaries is to turn off your phone during meals, allowing yourself to fully engage with the people around you. This small act allows you to be present in conversations, free from the constant temptation of notifications. Rather than sending reels, connect with your friends through meaningful conversations. By sharing personal stories, exchanging laughter, and being present with each other in the moment, we can create memories that last beyond likes and comments.

Another effective way to reduce digital-induced loneliness is to take a break from technology altogether. Consider dedicating one day each week to being free from social media. This could mean going on a "digital detox day" where you don't touch your phone or open your laptop, allowing you to reconnect with yourself and the world around you. Use this time to engage in activities that don't require posting online–things that help you feel grounded, like reading a book, cooking a meal for your family, or going for a walk.

By making conscious choices, we can stop ourselves from becoming more isolated in the digital space. One artsy sunrise photo can freeze a moment of beauty and invite others to see the world through your lens. But when the numbers–likes, shares, and comments–become the focus, the essence of that moment fades. So, instead of chasing validation, we can choose to appreciate the simple joy of capturing something meaningful.

Vlogging is an excellent way to have conversations with the world and share your perspective and experiences. But if your ring light sees you more often than your parents, your friends, your own reflection in the mirror, then it's time to step back. And yes, podcasts–those fascinating windows into the minds of brilliant thinkers–are excellent. However, this one-sided communication should never replace the depth of learning from a fellow human being sitting right beside you.

The choices are clear: **Will we let ourselves become human scrolls, endlessly lost in a digital maze, or will we choose to build meaningful connections that lift the weight of loneliness?** Every choice we make will determine whether the loneliness amplified by digital platforms becomes a permanent part of our lives or not.

CHOICE 2

FEAR OF JUDGMENT VS FREEDOM OF BEING YOURSELF

"Sometimes, people are lonely because they are afraid to be themselves. So, they pretend to be someone else, and then they get lonely because they're not being genuine."

– Billie Eilish

When I first arrived in South Korea in August 2024, it felt like I had stepped into a quieter and more disciplined world. The streets were spotless, as if they had just been swept moments ago. Every corner felt like a scene straight out of a K-drama. On the metro, the silence was striking. No chatter, no phones rang. Each person was moving in perfect rhythm with the world around them. In the heart of the massive city of Seoul, I could hear the sounds of nature, birds singing, leaves rustling, as if the city itself had paused to listen.

I couldn't imagine such silence in the streets of India. Both country was a stark contrast to each other. In India, if street vendors call out their wares on one corner, while on another, the beeping of horns and the hurried footsteps of people racing against time create a rhythm that is both chaotic and alive. In India, life doesn't whisper, it roars. It hits you with the rich smells of chole bhature and idli sambar, the lights of Diwali, and the colours of Holi. It's more than a country–it's a celebration of life, culture, people, and the beautiful chaos of being fully present.

Serene, structured streets mark one country, while the other country is alive with unorganised, vibrant energy. However, beneath the surface, I noticed one glaring similarity that binds these two countries together despite their outward contrasts: the weight of judgment.

Whether I find myself in a foreign country, grappling with an unfamiliar language and culture, or back home where everything should feel comforting and familiar, judgment seems to exist in both situations. Its weight is constant and universal, never loud or obvious, but always present, quietly watching, quietly measuring. Due to its chameleon nature, judgment adapts, changing its appearance to blend seamlessly with the culture, country, and context it inhabits. Yet, at its core, its true nature remains unchanged–it still divides, labels, and distances us from others.

Parasite, a 2019 South Korean film directed by Bong Joon-ho, took the world by storm. It garnered global praise, earning the Palme d'Or and four Academy Awards. But beyond its critical acclaim, the film offers a sharp commentary on societal divides. It highlights the subtle yet harsh ways in which people are judged, particularly along class lines in South Korea. The film explores how societal markers such as prestigious degrees, refined manners, and the way of speaking can dictate one's perceived value. It shows how something as simple as body odour can be used to label someone as lower class or poor, highlighting the emotional distance and lack of empathy the upper class feels toward them.

Parasite isn't just a film, it's a sharp critique of the unspoken rules that shape South Korean society. If you think the reality portrayed in Parasite is confined to just one country, then you're mistaken. It's a truth that stretches across every corner of the world. The class division, societal expectations, and the judgment based on one's background are universal. They cross borders and resonate with people all over the world.

Growing up, I was judged for being quiet and introverted. "Shy", "underconfident", "weak", "not smart enough"–those labels stuck to me like glue. In every environment, I saw everyone praising loud, bold personalities who could effortlessly grab attention and light up a room. At the same time, they would look at me and say, "If you stay quiet like this, you won't get anywhere as you grow up."

It felt like my quietness was something to be fixed. "Why can't I be like others?" This thought echoed in my head, growing louder and more persistent. The fear of judgment pushed me to mold myself into whatever shape I thought others wanted to see. But in doing so, I lost touch with who I really was.

Personality isn't the only thing people judge me on. In my life, judgment feels like that persistent, toxic friend who never truly disappears. It hangs in the background, quietly shaping my choices and experiences in ways I don't always see. From Bhubaneswar to Delhi, Kolkata to Bangalore, as I've moved from city to city for work or education, the feeling of never truly belonging to any culture has followed me every step of the way. Coming from the Northeast of India, where language, culture, and food are worlds apart from the rest of the country, I've encountered many questions regarding my culture and food habits. Sometimes, comments were lighthearted and curious, but other times, it felt like a stone in my chest–heavy and uncomfortable, highlighting just how different I am from what they consider "normal."

"Do you eat dogs?"

"Is it true that chowmein and momo are the only dishes your state has to offer?"

"Are you even Indian?"

Each question is a silent accusation that strips me of my identity. When people use these comments, they fail to realise it's not just about words; it's about the constant dehumanisation of those who don't fit the mainstream mold. Many from the Northeast face being called derogatory names like "Chinki" or "Chinese".[1] Such labels reflect the deep-seated prejudice and ignorance that still exist, reducing a rich, diverse culture of India to harmful stereotypes based solely on appearance or origin.

India is home to over 19,500 dialects and 121 languages, making it one of the most linguistically diverse countries in the world. The Indian government officially recognises 22 of these languages.[2] Yet, when I don't speak the dominant language of a state, I'm often met with subtle reactions that seem to ask, "Do you even belong here?"

In India, if the language shifts every 100 kilometres, then in every 200 kilometres, the cuisine and culture also change. Yet, when I choose to eat certain non-vegetarian foods during specific times of the month or festivals not observed in my hometown, it draws whispered comments and awkward silences from the local people. These reactions often make me question, "Am I committing a sin?" Cultural norms shape not only my actions but also how I am perceived, even in the most personal choices.

These judgments chipped away at my confidence. It wasn't just about what others thought of me–it was the constant fear of being seen for who I truly was. Society always has an unspoken blueprint – a set of milestones we're expected to reach by certain ages, as if these are the inevitable steps determining our success and happiness. The more you stray from these expected milestones, the louder the judgment becomes.

By the time I hit 30, I had become familiar with the questions that came up at every family gathering: "Why aren't you married yet?" as though my singlehood was a symptom of something broken, a sign that I had failed at a major life event. At 32, the script was updated: "Don't you want kids?" as if the absence of motherhood in my life was a looming crisis, an emotional fault line waiting to crack open and swallow me whole.

The questions often come disguised as harmless concern from "well-wishers," but deep down, they're just judgments wrapped in polite packaging. I wish I could say, "I don't care," and truly mean it. But the truth is, their words got under my skin. They made me question my worth, not because I believed them, but because I started comparing my life to the timeline society had mapped out for me. There is a part of me that wants to be seen just as I am–raw, honest, and without apology. But that desire is often shadowed by the fear of being judged.

Many would argue that the world has become more fluid and diverse, with globalisation and a growing emphasis on individuality encouraging acceptance and open-mindedness. However, no matter how much society evolves, it always seems to find a new way to judge each other. Today, society doesn't slap you in the face and say, "You're not good enough!" It just sits there, looking at you like a judgmental cat with a snarky smile, reminding you that no matter how far you've come, you still haven't quite arrived.

Caste-based discrimination, once a rigid system in many parts of the world, has now morphed into a more widespread form of classism. It's no longer about who you were born to but about how much you earn, what job you hold, how educated you are, and what kind of lifestyle you lead. Still, those in higher classes are often seen as more capable, deserving, and "better," while those in lower classes are burdened with stereotypes of being incapable. So, we keep chasing the next title, the next paycheck, the next piece of validation, wondering when we'll finally be seen as "enough".[3]

Today, your worth is often judged by what you own. Your phone, your car, your degree, and your clothes are all silent markers of your place in society. If you drive an SUV, you're practically elite. Your car is not just a vehicle, it's an image. If you're the person who shows up to work wearing sunglasses and making plans to hit up a fancy brunch on the weekend, then you are successful.

Meanwhile, if you roll up in a small car, it's like driving in with a neon sign that says, "I'm just getting by, folks."

Your choices to buy things may be practical and efficient, but in the eyes of classism, your sensible decision becomes a symbol of financial insecurity. Not just about material wealth; today, the name of the school or university you attend often outweighs the actual knowledge you gain.

I completed my schooling at a small government Assamese-medium school. At that time, my parents, both educators, believed that true education had nothing to do with the price tag of the institution. For them, it was about the values I gained. But I remember the first time someone in my engineering college asked me, "Where did you go to school?" and I proudly said, "I studied in a government Assamese medium school." Suddenly, the room seemed to fall silent, as if the words had the power to erase everything I'd worked for. And then came the looks–the unspoken judgment. One person raised an eyebrow; another looked at me with a mix of disbelief and pity. They seemed to place me in some invisible box, a place far removed from their own "elite" schools and "prestigious" education. At that moment, the value of my education was suddenly reduced to a label, to a stamp that said I was from a less "impressive" background.

It's funny how society, so self-proclaimed in its wisdom, feels it has the right to box us into categories. These boxes are often drawn without our consent, defining who we are and how we should be, leaving little room for individuality or authenticity. One of the most devastating ways society loves to box us is with mental health issues. Despite the progress we've made in opening up the conversation, mental health continues to be a battleground where societal judgment plays a powerful, harmful role. We're told to be "strong," to "just get over it," to bury our pain beneath a mask of normalcy, as if the struggles of the mind are somehow less valid than those of the body. But the truth is, mental health doesn't fit into the tidy boxes society tries to force on it. People who are going through mental health challenges are labelled as "weak," "unstable," or worse, "crazy," as if their humanity is up for debate.

Having navigated my own mental health challenges, I've come to understand that facing these battles within yourself is hard enough, but acknowledging them to others? That's even harder than we often imagine. A raw, vulnerable fear comes with opening up–a fear that others might not understand or, worse, that they'll judge you. When you're already fighting an invisible battle, the last thing you need is someone making you feel as if this struggle defines your worth.

But why? Why is it that every time society judges us, we start to question our self-worth? Why do the expectations of others weigh so heavily on our shoulders, as if our value depends on meeting their standards? Why does the idea of being cast aside or rejected for simply being ourselves feel so terrifying?

When Aristotle said, "Man is by nature a social animal," he suggested that humans are inherently inclined to live in communities and form connections with others. The idea of living in isolation feels unnatural, even though it may sometimes seem like the only escape from judgment. From the days of hunter-gatherers, where survival depended on cooperation and shared efforts, to today's modern nation-states, the essence of our progress and happiness has always been tied to our ability to form connections. Our survival, both as individuals and as a species, has always been linked to the strength of our relationships with one another.[4]

So, the truth is undeniable: we need society. We need people to accept us, pull us into their circles, and include us in their tribes. This is not just a desire for companionship; it's a fundamental need to belong, to be seen, and to matter. To get the chance to be seen in a world that tells us we're only worthy if we conform, we're often willing to wear a mask.

In ancient Greek theatre, actors wore masks, known as personae, to portray different characters, each one crafted to represent a specific role or identity. Over time, the term persona evolved, symbolising the social "mask" individuals wear in public to fit society's expectations. In his 16th-century political treatise "The Prince", Niccolò Machiavelli argued that rulers often had to wear a mask of virtue and morality despite their true, self-serving intentions. The mask, in essence, became a tool not just for survival but for power, revealing how deeply ingrained the need to conform and be accepted is in the human experience.[5]

Fast-forward to the Victorian era in the 19th century, a time of sweeping social change, industrialisation, and cultural refinement.[6] Yet it was also a period deeply rooted in stringent moral codes and a society that valued appearances above all else. In such an environment, people often found themselves "wearing masks" of propriety–presenting a polished, proper exterior that concealed their true feelings, desires, and identities. For women, this meant suppressing personal ambition, emotions, and even basic human desires in favour of idealised, passive femininity.[7]

Throughout every decade of history, whether shaped by social norms, systemic pressures, or the relentless drive to succeed, people have felt the need to wear masks, adjusting parts of themselves to meet society's expectations. Over time, this becomes our second nature: smile when you're sad, nod when you disagree, fit in even when it costs you authenticity. We become so accustomed to wearing the mask that we forget who we are beneath it. Indeed, the mask might help us feel accepted–but doesn't it also leave us feeling alone, even in a crowd?

Before we lose ourselves entirely, we must make a choice: **Will we continue to hide, to shrink, to pretend–simply because it's what's always been done? Or will we be the ones to break the pattern?**

The 'What Would People Say' Mentality Breeds Loneliness

"When we fit in instead of belonging, we mold ourselves to be acceptable, and in doing so, we fuel our loneliness."

– Brene Brown

"What would people say?" This common phrase acts as an invisible force that causes people to adopt choices and lifestyles that are at odds with their true personalities, desires, or even financial realities. One of the most glaring examples of this is the phenomenon of extravagant weddings, where families spend lavishly, not for personal joy, but to satisfy the thought, "What would people say?"

Weddings today aren't just about making memories; they're about making impressions. Indian weddings are already grand affairs, with long celebrations filled with detailed rituals, countless guests, and extravagant arrangements. But recently, there has been a shift towards destination weddings, with couples seeking to replicate the glamorous celebrations often seen in the lives of celebrities. Instead of following the rituals and essence of marriage, these weddings have transformed into meticulously curated, picture-perfect experiences, where every detail is planned to perfection in order to create an idealised version of the celebration.

But can everyone afford that? Families with significant wealth or high incomes may easily afford these arrangements without much financial strain, but they represent only a small percentage of income earners–about 10%. What about the majority of Indian families? The pressure to meet societal expectations pushes them to stretch beyond their means. The pressure to keep up with society's standards pushes many to dip into lifelong savings or borrow money, all for one day.

According to a report by Business Standard, approximately 20% of young Indians have taken loans to fund their weddings.[8] Many of them face difficulties repaying these loans, leading to ongoing financial burdens. The burden of paying off loans or sacrificing future needs can lead to frustration, regret, and even resentment. These wedding-related debts cause feelings of anxiety, stress, and financial regret. This is the story of every other middle-class family.

Similar to India, weddings in South Korea are often considered a way to showcase one's social status. Families may spend heavily on luxury venues, designer outfits, and expensive gifts for guests.[9] In the U.S., the "wedding industrial complex" promotes the idea that a wedding must be a once-in-a-lifetime, fairy-tale event. This has led to rising costs and unrealistic expectations.[10] All for a moment of applause, ignoring the lasting consequences that reveal the emptiness of such conformity.

The pressure to meet society's expectations extends far beyond weddings. It seeps into every aspect of life, crushing dreams daily. Another significant pressure stemming from the weight of "What would people say" is the drive to pursue prestigious careers–engineering, medicine, law–the so-called "safe" and "respectable" professions. These fields are often seen as the only acceptable paths to success and social approval, leaving little room for individuals to follow their own passions or interests.

The definition of a "safe" career may change over time, but it is always shaped by society. In the process, the true passions, dreams, and happiness of countless individuals are often overlooked and buried under the heavy weight of social expectations. It's like asking a fish to fly. No matter how hard it tries, it will never feel at home in the sky. The struggle to fit into a mold that wasn't made for us often leads to a life that feels out of sync with our true selves.

Over time, the disconnection from one's true passions and desires in a career gradually erodes confidence, replacing curiosity with frustration and self-doubt. The excitement that should come with pursuing a career turns into a sense of burdensome obligation. Every year, India sees a rise in mental health issues as more individuals find themselves in careers that conflict with their nature, intensifying feelings of isolation and dissatisfaction.

Gender stereotypes add yet another layer to the struggle of "What would people say?" by defining which careers are considered "appropriate" for men and women, further limiting individual choice and potential.[11] As a mechanical engineer, I've seen raised eyebrows and skeptical looks when people hear about my engineering field. Mechanical engineering, still largely viewed as a "masculine" field, is thought to require physical strength and technical skills that, according to some, women supposedly lack. In many interviews, I was rejected not because I lacked the ability or knowledge, but simply because I was a girl.

On the other hand, careers like nursing or therapy are often labelled as "feminine" due to their association with caregiving and empathy. Many men who are genuinely passionate about these fields hesitate to pursue them, not because they lack the ability or interest, but because society insists they should aim for something "more manly." The pressure to conform to gendered expectations can be just as stifling and limiting for men as it is for women.

These judgments don't just shape careers; they shape lives. Before dreams are crushed, passions are buried, and choices are dictated by fear, our individuality is the first casualty in this process. We sacrifice our uniqueness and internal compass, prioritising external approval over our true desires, passions and sense of purpose. Often, it's the result of Herd Mentality–a psychological phenomenon where individuals adopt the beliefs, behaviours or attitudes of a group, often suppressing their own judgment in the process.[12] We fear falling out of step with the crowd so deeply that, even when no one is directly saying anything, we still feel an internal pressure, driven by the fear of missing out (FOMO) or the deep desire to be accepted.

Take the example of buying a new phone–sleek, shiny, and packed with the same features your old one already had. Why do you do it? Because celebrities flaunt it. Your friends have it. Your colleague has it. You feel the need to keep up. In your mind, owning it makes you part of an elite group.

Then comes the wardrobe overhaul. Maybe it's a shiny new pair of shoes, a designer handbag, or that stylish jacket you saw everyone else wearing. It's no longer about practicality or comfort; it's about making a statement. A statement that says, "I belong. I am part of something bigger." You start to associate your worth with the things you own, believing they define you.

Society might applaud the version of yourself you've chosen to present, but the constant choices we make every day to impress others only deepen that feeling of isolation. Carl Rogers, a humanistic psychologist, explored this tension between the "real self", who we truly are, and the "ideal self", who we think we should be based on societal expectations.[13] He emphasised that the effort to maintain the facade, to pretend to be someone else, is mentally and emotionally draining.

We experience a sense of incongruence–a gap that can lead to anxiety, low self-esteem, and emotional exhaustion. From a neuroscience perspective, the consequences of in authenticity are profound. When we are being inauthentic, Ventral Striatum, the part of the brain responsible for the pleasure we experience from genuine interactions, doesn't get activated. As a result, we experience a kind of emptiness, even when surrounded by a crowd of people. This disconnection also affects our Default Mode Network (DMN), the brain system responsible for self-reflection. When we're not being our true selves, our brain struggles to understand who we really are, leading to confusion about our identity and further increasing feelings of loneliness. It's like trying to connect with others while holding a mask up between you and them.[14]

So, before choosing to be the person shaped by the pressure of "What would people say?", we must ask ourselves: Is the choice of seeking acceptance really worth the cost of losing our authenticity?

For years, I wore the mask of an extrovert, convinced it was the only way to avoid being alone. I harnessed all my strengths as an introvert–my deep thinking, quiet creativity, and ability to form connections that went beyond superficial conversations. Why? Because I believed that if I didn't fit into a society that praised outgoing and loud, I would become invisible. I told myself, "If I can fake it, I'll finally belong."

But the truth is, pretending was never worth what it took from me. I was drained after every small conversation, exhausted by the constant effort of being someone I wasn't. Inside, I felt empty, under confident, and worn out–like there was a hole that nothing could fill. There were moments when I saw myself as a failure. I just wanted to disappear, to shrink away from it all and hide in the corner of a cupboard, far from the world and the relentless pressure to be something I wasn't.

Isn't it ironic? In trying to escape loneliness and silence the fear of "what would people say," I began pretending. Yet, it was this very act of pretending that deepened my loneliness, pulling me further from myself and anything genuine or real.

Lao Tzu, the ancient Chinese philosopher, once said, "Care about what other people think, and you will always be their prisoner." And he was right. When we live according to others' expectations, we become prisoners of their judgment, shackled by the constant pressure to conform. Our thoughts are consumed by what others may think, drowning out our own sense of self-worth. In this cycle of self-doubt, loneliness thrives because no matter how many people surround us, we remain disconnected from our own truth.

But what happens if we stop conforming? At first, there may be discomfort. Society might judge us, gossip about us, and whisper behind our backs. We may be the talk of the town for a moment, but like an old newspaper discarded and forgotten the day after it was printed, our efforts to conform will fade away just as quickly. The performance we put on to fit in will have no lasting impact. What will remain, however, is the life we sacrificed in the endless pursuit of pleasing others.

In the past, it's not that we didn't care about what society thought– we did. Even then, we made compromises, sometimes silencing our true selves to fit in the mold. But the scale was smaller, and the reach was limited. The sad truth is that, despite all our talk of progress, despite the masks of rebellion and advancement we now wear, the core struggle hasn't changed. Today, it's not just those around us setting expectations–it's influencers curating perfect lives, advertisements selling happiness in a bottle, and algorithms feeding us a constant stream of "what you should be." Whether directly or subtly, we're told what happiness should look like–what to wear, where to be, and who to become–all in pursuit of one haunting concern: "What would people say?"

Do I look good enough to be liked if I share this picture? Should I switch to a new company like everyone else? Are they thinking I'm less happy because I haven't travelled anywhere this year? If I buy this house in this complex, will they think I'm not financially sound? These questions are like playing a game of charades, where you're desperately trying to guess the right moves. The pressure to measure up to these standards can be overwhelming, leaving us feeling disconnected and adrift, uncertain of who we truly are.

Loneliness won't disappear as long as we keep asking ourselves, "What would people say?" In fact, it only grows louder–amplified by the pressure to match idealised lives that were never meant to reflect our reality. But the choice still lies with us: **Will we continue to follow someone else's script, trying to live up to an image that was never truly ours? Or will we choose to live a life that's true rather than performative?**

Let's Embrace Who We Are

"Loneliness is not a lack of people, but the absence of self."

– Irwin D. Yalom

Picture a middle-class family that no longer feels the need to hide their struggles by stretching their budget just to keep up appearances. Instead of buying things to impress others, they choose to invest in what truly matters to them–things they've always dreamed of, not because they need validation, but because they've earned it. They no longer feel inferior when someone tries to put them down or judge their choices. Instead, they stand tall, showing the kind of confidence that says, "I'm proud of how far I've come. I'll keep showing up and moving forward."

Imagine a world where introverts don't have to shout to matter, where their quiet strength and thoughtful presence are finally recognised as powerful. Picture a world where extroverts don't tone down their natural energy or feel guilty for wanting the spotlight but step into it unapologetically, their enthusiasm sparking joy in others.

Imagine a society where people don't shy away from their traditions or feel hesitant to speak their mother tongue. A world where another culture's customs aren't judged but welcomed, where diversity isn't something to tolerate, but something to celebrate.

These worlds aren't some far-off fantasy of mixed reality. It's within our reach, waiting to be built with every choice we make to learn, to share, and to connect. The question isn't if it's possible–it's whether we're brave enough to take that first step and decide to embrace our true selves without having the fear of "What would people say?"

When we stop apologising for who we are, we show the world that authenticity is the true definition of beauty. There are remarkable figures in history who changed the world simply because they refused to wear a mask. Ratan Tata, the renowned industrialist and philanthropist, is a powerful example of someone who stayed true to his values instead of getting swept up in the pursuit of public validation. Despite heading one of the world's largest business empires, he often shared glimpses of his quiet, introspective personality–something that might seem unexpected in a world that equates leadership with loud confidence. His calm, thoughtful presence stood out in an era of self-promotion, reminding us that strength doesn't always need to shout.[15]

Similarly, Barack Obama's journey to becoming a charismatic leader was rooted in embracing authenticity. One of the pivotal moments that truly defined his leadership was his keynote speech at the 2004 Democratic National Convention. Rather than trying to mimic other successful political figures or fit into a certain mold, Obama spoke from the heart about unity, hope, and the potential for change. He didn't try to adopt a pre-packaged political persona; he leaned into his unique experiences as a biracial, thoughtful leader with a deep connection to the challenges faced by everyday people.[16]

Throughout his career, Obama stressed the importance of introspection, admitting his faults, and allowing himself to be vulnerable. He was upfront about his past struggles, including his battles with identity and his journey of self-discovery. This honesty allowed him to connect with people on a deeper level, and over time, it shaped his image as a leader who could be trusted to lead with intellect and empathy. His authenticity became the foundation of his charisma.

Could Ratan Tata and Barack Obama have earned the respect of millions if they had pretended to be someone they're not or chased approval? Definitely not. The world has always celebrated those who are brave enough to embrace their imperfections, who refuse to blend into the background.

Embracing your true self often feels like standing alone in a crowd, like swimming against a relentless tide. But that's the first step in creating authentic relationships. When you embrace who you truly are, you attract the people who truly understand you, who value you for the right reasons. In a world that can often feel isolating, it's the people who see you for exactly who you are–your flaws, your strengths, and everything in between- that make all the difference.

Society pushes us toward sameness, urging us to fit into predefined molds, follow well-worn paths, and wear the same masks as everyone else. To step out of that stream and say, "This is who I am," isn't just a choice–it's a quiet act of rebellion against the pressures to conform, against the loud voices that try to shape us into someone we're not.

So, are you ready for that rebellion?

This answer will change everything. Maybe the path of pretending is easy, and embracing your authentic self is tough. But pretending promises hollow acceptance, one laced with loneliness and the broken pieces of your authenticity.

It took me years to face the truth that I had depression. I hid it, buried it deep within, pretending it wasn't there. The stigma around mental health issues made me believe that if I didn't talk about it, no one would see how broken I felt. I was terrified that if I did open up, those who loved me might look at me as less than whole. So I kept quiet, carrying that weight alone, convinced that silence would somehow make it better.

But the truth is, it didn't make anything better. It only made me more isolated. The more I tried to bury my pain, the more I felt myself slipping away from everyone around me–until the loneliness became my permanent companion. Then, one day, everything changed. I hit a point where I could no longer deny it. I couldn't hide anymore. And in that moment, I decided, "I'm done pretending. It's time to accept this for what it is."

That was the turning point. Accepting my depression didn't make me weak–it made me stronger than I ever thought possible. I didn't fall apart as I feared. Instead, I found support from the people who loved me, from those who had been silently waiting for me to open up. It was like a weight lifted off my shoulders, and in its place, something new began to grow.

From the depths of my darkness, I planted the seed for something that would carry me forward–"Ready2Live". It is a platform to reach thousands of people like me–those quietly struggling with their mental health, afraid to speak, afraid to be seen. Its purpose is simple: to educate, to raise awareness, and it's okay to have mental health issues. It is nothing to be ashamed of. Just like any physical illness, mental health issues deserve care, understanding, and compassion. Through "Ready2Live", I've had the chance to share not just my story, but my strength–and in doing so, help others find theirs too. I realised that sharing my authentic self wasn't about showing weakness; it was about showing the world that the most powerful thing we can do is let ourselves be seen, exactly as we are.

I wish, looking back, I could take back those years of pretending. Those years of editing myself, hiding the parts that felt too raw, too real. One of the main reasons that stops us from being authentic isn't just the judgment from society; it's also the judgment that comes from within. Sometimes we are our own harshest critics, constantly questioning if we're enough, if we're doing it right, or if we'll be accepted. "Why can't I just be more social like him?" or "What's wrong with me?" These thoughts create a loop of self-doubt, making it harder to feel good about ourselves.

The real problem with these self-critical thoughts is that they fixate on what we believe is "wrong" with us, while ignoring the things that make us unique and valuable. Nobody is perfect. Not your colleagues who got that promotion ahead of you, or your neighbours who just drove by in the latest SUV. Perfection is a matter of perspective. It's about how we choose to see ourselves and others. We can either focus on imperfections and shortcomings, or we can embrace the beauty of our individuality–both the flaws and the strengths. The choice is ours.

In the moments of self-judgment, it's important to pause and ask, "Would I ever say this to a friend?" It's easy to be harsh with ourselves, but we often forget that the same kindness we extend to others is what we need most. We're usually far more forgiving and compassionate with the people we care about than we are with ourselves. But in those times when we feel down or unsure, we deserve that same level of care. This also doesn't mean ignoring our weaknesses or the areas where we want to improve; instead, it means approaching these areas with kindness and curiosity rather than harsh judgment.

There is a golden rule here: We must first see the beauty in our own authenticity. This isn't just about feel-good clichés–it's backed by data. Studies in emotional intelligence show that those who embrace vulnerability tend to have better interpersonal relationships and greater self-awareness. When we approach our flaws with curiosity instead of judgment, we're more likely to learn from them and evolve.

Vulnerability isn't a weakness. In fact, it's often the bravest thing we can do. Back in the early days of psychology, being vulnerable was seen as a sign of insecurity or emotional instability. It was something to avoid, something that made people seem fragile. But then came the humanistic psychology movement, with figures like Carl Rogers and Abraham Maslow, who flipped that idea on its head. They started to emphasise the importance of being authentic and accepting ourselves for who we really are–something that often means embracing vulnerability. They showed us that being real, even when it's messy or uncomfortable, is actually a strength. Vulnerability is the gateway to connection, self-acceptance, and personal growth.[17]

Brené Brown, a researcher renowned for her work on vulnerability, reminds us that our willingness to be vulnerable actually fosters courage, creativity, and meaningful connections. Her research shows that vulnerability is at the core of building trust and connection. When we allow ourselves to be vulnerable, we stop hiding behind walls of fear and start making room for authenticity to flourish.

So, yes, even when you feel like a chaotic whirlwind, spinning uncontrollably in all directions–remember this: embracing vulnerability means understanding that growth doesn't come from avoiding discomfort, but from leaning into it.

Embracing our authentic selves is a journey, full of twists and turns. It asks us to peel away the years of labels, roles, and expectations. It's a process that demands courage, requiring us to confront the fears that have kept us in hiding. What if we're rejected? What if we're not enough? What if being ourselves means standing alone? To walk this path, we have to let those "what ifs" go and embrace the truth that it's okay to be exactly who you are. And in doing so, we make room for something extraordinary: the freedom to be real, the strength to be authentic, and the beauty of simply being ourselves.

So choice is: **Will we be honest, not just with the world, but with the quiet, tender truth that lives within us?Or will we**

keep hiding behind the mask, hoping it will protect us from judgment?

Before you decide, remember this: We can't let the longing for approval lead us into loneliness. We must not let it drown out the quiet voice that gently whispers, "You are beautiful, exactly as you are." Your truth isn't a flaw–it's your strength. It's your power.

What Can We Do as a Society?

"The more you judge, the less you love."

– Honore de Balzac

In 1901, Rabindranath Tagore, the renowned Indian poet, philosopher, and social reformer, founded Shantiniketan with a vision of something far beyond the boundaries of a typical educational institution. His dream was not just to create a school but to craft an environment where students from all backgrounds –rich and poor, Hindu and Muslim, urban and rural–could come together to study and grow in an atmosphere of equality, mutual respect, and shared humanity. At Shantiniketan, students were encouraged to engage with each other beyond the labels of their social, cultural or religious identities.[18]

Tagore dreamed of a world where humanity was at the heart of everything. He imagined a place free from fear, prejudice, and hatred, where understanding and kindness guided our actions. He wished for a world where people could look past their differences and see the shared humanity in each other's eyes.

Now, in the 21st century, we pat ourselves on the back for all our progress. But let's be real–has Tagore's vision truly come to life? Or have we just gotten better at masking our biases with hashtags? If we're still judging people for the way they dress, speak, or eat, then what's really changed? The same old patterns of judgment and division are still alive–just wrapped in a new, modern package.

In our rush to celebrate individual success, we've lost sight of what truly matters. We've forgotten that the kind of progress that transforms societies isn't measured by personal achievements alone. It's measured by what we choose to face together–the biases we're willing to unlearn, the judgments we replace with empathy, and the understanding we offer instead of turning away.

The first step in creating a judgment-free world is recognising that, despite our differences, we are all human. We may come from different walks of life, have different personalities, have different financial stability or be raised in contrasting cultures, but at the core, we share the same struggles, same fears, and same hopes. Imagine, just for a moment, what could happen if we redirected even half the energy we spend on criticism into acts of kindness. Instead of scrutinising what's "different," what if we choose to embrace the beauty of diversity with open arms?

As a society, we have the power to create a world where judgment is left at the door and humanity takes the spotlight. But how do we get there? Let's begin with education. We need to educate ourselves and our younger generations to embrace diverse cultures, backgrounds, and perspectives to break down the biases that fuel judgment. While the world is obsessed with IQ and academic achievements, we must also prioritise emotional intelligence.

Emotional intelligence (EQ) is the key to truly understanding and feeling what others experience.[19]And it is something that should be nurtured from home, as it lays the foundation for building stronger, more compassionate connections with those around us. Right now, our society struggles with understanding each other, connecting with one another, and truly empathising with different experiences. A perfect example of this is the rising cases of bullying. A study by the NCPCR indicated that 42% of school students in India have experienced bullying - a number that can't be easily ignored. And it doesn't stop at school. Cyberbullying is also becoming a major issue. A 2021 McAfee study found that 85% of Indian kids have faced cyberbullying, the highest rate of any country surveyed.[20]

The negative effects of bullying are often far more severe than we realise. It can have a lasting impact on a child's mental health, damaging their self-esteem and making them feel undeserving of friendship or love. It can hinder the development of social skills, making it harder for victims to form meaningful relationships. As a result, many experience loneliness from an early age, and it often continues into adulthood. A 2019 study in *The Lancet Psychiatry* revealed the alarming reality that children subjected to bullying face a two to three times greater risk of self-harm or suicide attempts.[21]

So, what's driving this vicious cycle?

Bullying often stems from power imbalances, where individuals or groups assert dominance over those perceived as "weaker" or "different." When children grow up in a society where mocking someone's accent or judging a family member for the way they dress is disturbingly normalised, they absorb those behaviours. They see it happening around them, and often, they start repeating it.

Bullying doesn't occur in a vacuum–it reflects the broader judgments and values of the society around it. So the question isn't "Why are kids so cruel?" but "What are we doing to stop it?" Teaching children kindness, empathy, and respect should never be optional. These values are just as essential as math or science. When we raise children to choose understanding over judgment, we help shape a culture rooted in compassion rather than cruelty. If children witness accountability–where unkindness is called out rather than ignored–they learn that respect should never be conditional.

To create a judgment-free world, we, as a society, must understand that it's not our role to be gatekeepers, dictating how others should live or handing out a one-size-fits-all blueprint for life. We must resist the urge to reduce people to labels or stereotypes and instead recognise the full complexity of who they truly are. We need to stop measuring success by a single, fixed destination or basing our worth on comparisons with others. If someone chooses not to marry, that decision should be respected. Similarly, if someone prioritises their family, they shouldn't be judged as less of a feminist. Each person's choices, whether they align with societal expectations or not, reflect their individuality and should be celebrated, not criticised.

The solution is straightforward: let's build a world where kindness tears down societal judgment. And no, it's not rocket science! Sometimes, all it takes is one person and one small gesture to remind someone they're not alone. When someone from Northeast India feels out of sync with the North Indian culture around them, we shouldn't make them feel out of place. Instead, we should make an effort to include them. Just because they don't immediately fit into the cultural norm doesn't mean they lack value. It just means they might need more time, understanding, and encouragement to feel at home and show the unique flavour they bring to the table.

Maybe our brains are wired to judge others' lifestyles. But kindness has the power to change everything. When you see someone struggling, ask yourself: What if you could be the support they need? That one small act could break the cycle of isolation and give someone the strength to keep going.

This shift in perspective isn't something that happens overnight. It starts with a decision we must make–together. So the choice is: **Will we take that first step–to truly see one another and begin letting go of the judgment? Or will we keep the door closed, and miss the chance to live in a world where we all feel like we belong–just as we are?**

CHOICE 3

EMPATHY VS EMOTIONAL ABSENCE

"Too often we underestimate the power of a touch, a smile, a kind word, a listening ear, an honest compliment, or the smallest act of caring, all of which have the potential to turn a life around."

– Leo Buscaglia

"I don't feel okay these days," I confessed, my voice trembling as I finally put into words the weight I had been carrying for months. It was December 2018 when I finally found the courage to open up to my flatmate about how I had been feeling. She wasn't just my flatmate; she was a friend I'd known since college, someone who had walked beside me for five years through every high and low. She'd seen me laugh until I cried and cry until I couldn't breathe. Midnight snacks, heartbreaks, last-minute deadlines, random celebrations for nothing, she had seen every version of me.

And yet, when things started falling apart inside me, I pulled away. "Would she understand what I was going through?" This question twisted inside me, tightening the grip, making it impossible to say the words, "I'm not feeling well. I need help."

It took everything in me to believe that if I let my guard down, if I finally shared what I was holding inside, I might find relief. That maybe, just maybe, someone would understand. And I was right. That day, when I finally opened up, she didn't rush me or judge me. She simply sat beside me and said, "I'm here to listen, to sit with you, and to help in whatever way feels right for you. You are not alone in this."

Her words didn't just comfort me. They made me feel seen, understood, and a little less alone. For the first time in a long while, I felt a spark of hope, something I had convinced myself was out of reach. And that hope gave me the courage to take the first step toward healing: booking my first therapy session.

My experience with depression felt like a silent battle. It was a force that turned my mind against itself, distorting my thoughts and making everything feel like a threat, especially the things I once found joy in. Depression whispered that isolation was the only way to protect myself, convincing me that pulling away from the world was my safest choice.

But through it all, I discovered something I never expected: the quiet strength of empathy. During my journey, empathy showed me the healing power of human connection. If depression kept telling me to resist reaching out, to push away any possibility of connection, then empathy showed me that I wasn't alone in my battle. If depression told me I wasn't worthy of love and was lowering my self-esteem, then empathy reminded me that there were people around me who cared deeply for me.

Would I have made it out of depression without the empathy my friend showed me from the very beginning? Maybe. Or maybe not. But one thing I know for sure, my journey would have been far more challenging.

The meaning of empathy is simple. It's the act of feeling what someone else feels and truly understanding their emotions. It is the universal glue that keeps us connected to our shared humanity. It allows us to form deeper relationships, build trust, and create a sense of community. Whether it's offering a comforting word to a friend in need or acting with kindness toward a stranger, empathy helps break down barriers and foster mutual understanding.[1]

In the early 1990s, researchers led by Giacomo Rizzolatti made a groundbreaking discovery that would profoundly change our understanding of human behaviour and emotional connection. While studying brain activity in monkeys at the University of Parma in Italy, Rizzolatti's team made an unexpected discovery. Some neurons fired when the monkeys performed specific actions, like picking an object, and when they watched another monkey perform the same action. These neurons, later named mirror neurons, appeared to "mirror" the actions of others.[2]

The discovery of mirror neurons, initially in monkeys and later in humans, has opened a fascinating window into the neural mechanisms behind human empathy. In essence, mirror neurons allowed our brain to "resonate" with others' emotions and behaviours, creating a neurological foundation for understanding and sharing emotional experiences. This ability to emotionally resonate with others is so powerful that witnessing someone's tears can evoke a sense of sadness in us, even if their situation doesn't directly impact us. Similarly, when we witness someone in joy, our own feelings of happiness may arise.[3]

This innate ability to mirror others is an automatic, unconscious process that helps us connect and empathise with those around us effortlessly. Yet the way people respond to and engage with others' emotions can vary greatly. Individual personalities, gender, and emotional intelligence mainly shape it. Some people are often more vocal and may express empathy through words. They might use physical gestures like hugs, pats on the back, or holding hands to convey their support and understanding.[4] On the other hand, introverts often excel at listening. They may show empathy by giving their full attention, maintaining eye contact, and nodding to acknowledge the other person's feelings. They may prefer to express empathy through writing, such as sending a heartfelt letter or message that conveys their support and understanding.

Gender can also shape how empathy is expressed. My husband's approach to showing empathy is completely different from mine. While I tend to express empathy through conversation and words, he takes a more hands-on approach. He jumps in, offering practical help when someone needs it, while I prefer to listen first before offering a solution. We may go about it differently, but at the heart of it, we are both trying to provide emotional support.

One of the most natural aspects of empathy is that we rarely think twice about offering it when someone's pain is visible.[5] Whether it's a loved one struggling with mental health issues or someone mourning the loss of a family member, when the suffering becomes clear, extending a listening ear or a helping hand feels instinctive. In those moments, empathy doesn't feel like a choice.

But what about the times when life seems "normal", when there are no major events, no obvious signs of pain or struggle? Are we truly empathetic during those times as well? Or do we tell ourselves that empathy is only necessary when someone explicitly asks for help? Have we ever made empathy a choice, often overshadowed by our daily distractions, personal struggles, and the fast pace of modern life?

Let's pause for a moment and think it over. When did you last sit with a friend, not just as a passive listener to their problems, but as someone who genuinely felt their pain or joy with them? Consider the introverted colleague who is quietly struggling to fit in. How many times have you reached out to them, made a conscious effort to include them or just acknowledged their presence in a way that made them feel seen and valued? If someone is dressed differently for a public event, do you make fun of them, even if it's just in your head? Or do you extend a hand, offer a word of kindness, or share a quiet moment that lets them feel a little less out of place? Have you ever stopped to help someone from a different culture who may not understand all the unspoken rules of your social circle or who might need a little warmth to feel like they belong?

Your responses to these questions will show whether you make empathy an optional choice in your lives, or if it still comes to you naturally. In our self-centred lives, prioritising productivity, achievement, and personal success over emotional connection is easy. Excuses like "I was too busy to notice" or "They'll figure it out on their own" reflect how much empathy has slipped away from our daily lives.

There was a time when people truly noticed each other, living in small towns or villages. Neighbours greeted each other in the morning, and the whole village felt like one big family. But over time, things started to shift. People moved to big cities and became disconnected from their roots and culture. Eyes are now glued to screens instead of meeting others face-to-face, conversations have grown shorter, and silence replaces the laughter that once filled crowded spaces. People began passing each other like ghosts, lost in their own thoughts, worries, and little worlds. We become less inclined to help strangers, less likely to look up from our own lives.[6] Studies have found that today's youth score significantly lower on empathy compared to the previous generations.[7]

Workplaces and communities also now suffer from a lack of genuine human connection as people prioritise efficiency over emotional bonds. A study conducted in 2022 by a Gallup poll found that 67% of employees reported feeling "disconnected" from their colleagues, citing productivity-focused environments as barriers to empathy.[8]

Digital technology, urbanisation, or capitalism–many people point to different reasons for the decline in empathy, but the main reason is that we often take empathy for granted. When it comes to mindfulness, we know that meditation is essential to quiet the mind. Similarly, maintaining good health means understanding the importance of regular exercise and not skipping it. But empathy is different. It develops so naturally through our daily interactions that we don't even recognise it as something we're actively "building."

You can witness empathy in a baby who instinctively feels the distress of another infant crying and joins in. As young as twelve months, they display rudimentary helping behaviours, indicating an early-emerging empathetic capacity. It's present in a toddler who notices someone's sadness and waddles over to offer a comforting hug. In high school students, empathy appears when they sit beside an overwhelmed classmate, silently sharing the weight of their stress. A college graduate shows empathy by listening attentively to a friend facing job rejection, gently reminding them of their worth. It's in the parent who consoles a heartbroken teenager, sharing stories of their own pain to show understanding. In the elderly, empathy is seen in their quiet act of holding someone's hand, offering silent strength to help them face grief.[9]

If empathy is so easily available, why do we still need to actively develop it? Because in the race for promotions, the chase to upgrade our lifestyles, earn higher salaries, or master the latest technologies, we often let emotional connections and empathy fall by the wayside or dismiss them as unnecessary. But here's the hard truth: Without empathy, nothing really matters. It's tempting to think that just having people around us can cure loneliness, but without empathy, those relationships can become empty distractions, masking the deeper ache we feel inside.

When Barack Obama said, "Empathy is a character trait capable of transforming the world," he highlighted a superpower that most of us fail to recognise in our everyday lives. This "superpower" isn't exclusive to the few; it's available to everyone from every background, if and only if we choose to nurture it. In a time when loneliness is spreading rapidly, empathy goes beyond being a simple virtue; it has become essential for making the world a better place for everyone. So the question is: **Will we continue to look past each other in silence, or will we choose to lean in, to listen, and to show empathy?**

Where Empathy Fades, Loneliness Grows

"Empathy fuels connection;
judgment fuels disconnection."

– Brene Brown

On one side, the rare warmth of empathy from a few people helped me crack open the silence around my depression. On the other hand, emotional neglect from others carved deeper wounds. Every time someone looked away or changed the subject, it felt like they were saying the same thing:

"Only speak to those who truly understand you."

"You're just overthinking–there's no real reason for you to feel this way."

"Why are you even sad? Other people have it way worse."

"Come on, stop thinking so much. You're making a problem where there isn't one."

"Just hit the gym. You're not exercising–that's why you feel like this."

"Maybe if you kept yourself busier, you wouldn't have time to feel like this."

These gaslighting remarks, the subtle disbelief, slowly constructed a wall around me, brick by brick, until I felt more isolated than ever. Some of my closest friends vanished, turning the conversation back to themselves with, "Let's talk about my problems instead." A few did listen, but only briefly, like they were fulfilling an obligation before moving on. Their ears heard me, but their hearts never really stayed.

Was I expecting some grand act of support? No, I didn't need someone to fix me. I just wanted to be heard, to feel even a fraction of the empathy. But as the lack of empathy continued, some tiny cracks began to form in the foundation of my relationships with them. Over time, those minor fractures deepened, slowly building a disconnection that grew harder and harder to ignore.

Imagine an adolescent feeling overwhelmed by intense emotions like mood swings, peer pressure, identity struggles, anxiety, or rebellion. They turn to their parent for reassurance, hoping for comfort or guidance. But instead, they're met with, "You're just being dramatic. Stop complaining." Or maybe the parent is too busy to really listen, brushing off their feelings as unimportant.

In that moment, the child feels unseen, unheard, and unsupported. When this happens again and again, they begin to believe that their emotions don't matter. Slowly, they start to withdraw, suppress their feelings, and build walls around themselves. Eventually, even in a house full of people, they can end up feeling completely alone.

It's easy to overlook the small moments from childhood, brushing them off as unimportant. But those early feelings, if left unresolved, quietly shape how we relate to others as adults. In 1969, British psychiatrist John Bowlby introduced a concept known as "Attachment Theory". It was a groundbreaking idea that the bonds children form with their primary caregivers lay the foundation for how they connect with others throughout their lives. Bowlby believed that from birth, we have an instinctual drive to build deep emotional connections, bonds that are essential not just for survival, but for feeling safe and growing emotionally.[10]

When children grow up feeling loved and supported, they develop a secure attachment, allowing them to explore the world confidently. But when their emotional needs are met with inconsistency, neglect, or indifference, they learn not to trust connections. This insecurity follows them into adulthood, shaping their relationships and even how they experience loneliness.

From childhood to adulthood, the need for emotional presence and empathy in relationships is a fundamental aspect of human connection. When we don't receive the emotional support we need from our partner, it's natural to start pulling away. Imagine you opening up to your partner about feeling overwhelmed by work.

You hope to be understood, but instead, your partner responds with, "You're always overreacting. Everyone has tough days. Just get over it." Such a response makes you feel dismissed and unimportant. You start to question yourself, and even the foundation of your relationship, "If the person I love doesn't understand me, then who will?" This belief can lead you to withhold more and more of your feelings, slowly building a wall between yourself and your partner.

John Gottman, a psychologist with a deep curiosity about relationships, was determined to understand what made some marriages flourish while others crumbled. His fascination led him to dedicate decades of research to uncovering the secrets of lasting love. Much of this groundbreaking research took place in what became known as Gottman's "Love Lab," a specially designed space where he observed couples in real time. He closely examined thousands of couples and their interactions, measuring not just their words but also their physiological responses, such as heart rate and skin conductance. This enabled Gottman to track the subtle yet powerful ways emotions influenced the course of their relationships over time.[11]

Through years of research, Gottman uncovered a powerful truth about relationships: emotional connection is the heart of a strong and healthy marriage. He discovered that couples who remained emotionally connected by being empathetic, understanding, and responsive were far more likely to build lasting, meaningful relationships. This deep bond didn't just help them face challenges together; it actually made their connection grow stronger over time.

Emotional neglect in our everyday interactions can accumulate, leading to a deeper sense of loneliness that has nothing to do with being alone in a room, but everything to do with feeling emotionally distant from those around us. A coworker who doesn't acknowledge your efforts, a friend who scrolls through their phone instead of listening to you, or a stranger who ignores your greeting–these are seemingly insignificant moments in everyday life. But these tiny lapses in empathy have a subtle yet powerful impact on our sense of connection and belonging.

Now, let's dive into the science to see the link between empathy and loneliness. When we receive empathy, something remarkable happens within our brain. The Anterior Cingulate Cortex (ACC) activates to help process our emotional pain. In that moment, it feels like our distress is truly being acknowledged. The weight of our feelings lightens, and for a brief second, the storm in our mind calms. While the Anterior Insula (AI) helps us stay present with those feelings, the Ventromedial Prefrontal Cortex (vmPFC) simultaneously gets to work, generating a sense of safety and support. We feel secure, as if the world around us momentarily becomes a little less harsh. Over time, positive and caring experiences help our brains feel good about connecting with others, making us want to keep building those bonds. This neural interplay doesn't just soothe us momentarily; it helps build resilience against loneliness by strengthening our sense of belonging.[12]

There's also another explanation of how empathy and loneliness are connected. When empathy is present, our brains release oxytocin, often called the "love hormone." It's what helps us feel safe, connected, and understood. Oxytocin plays a key role in regulating our emotions, building trust, and deepening our social bonds. But when empathy is missing, especially in moments of high stress, our brains respond in ways that make everything harder. Oxytocin drops. Meanwhile, cortisol, the stress hormone, surges. This imbalance causes a chain reaction where stress intensifies, our ability to connect with others diminishes, and we begin to pull away. The more isolated we become, the heavier the stress feels, locking us into a cycle of emotional fatigue and deepening loneliness.[13]

Empathy helps us manage our emotional pain, but more than that, it helps us to create a real sense of connection. Daniel Goleman, a renowned psychologist, highlights this in his book *Emotional Intelligence.* He mentioned that empathy isn't just a soft skill; it's a vital force that shapes our relationships, our well-being, and the fabric of society itself. He explains that when empathy is absent, our brains don't just register emotional pain–they react as if we're being physically hurt. Imagine the ache of feeling misunderstood or rejected; it's not only in your heart but sometimes felt as a real, aching pain in your body. This powerful connection between our emotions and physical sensations shows just how deeply our minds and bodies are intertwined, reminding us that emotional wounds can cut as deeply as physical ones.[14]

Empathy benefits not only those who receive it but also transforms those who give it. Often, empathy leads to altruistic behaviour, where we act to benefit others. This can create a cycle of reciprocal altruism, where others are more likely to respond with empathy and support in return. Receiving empathy helps us feel seen and connected. But when we show empathy to someone, we enrich our own sense of belonging, too. It is an emotional currency–the more we invest, the more we gain.[15]

That's the beauty of empathy. It's not just a selfless act - it's a shared experience that enriches both the giver and the receiver. This mutual exchange can also shift our focus away from our own loneliness. By concentrating on the needs and feelings of others, we momentarily step outside our own isolation, creating a sense of belonging and relief.

Studies, researchers, and philosophers have repeatedly shown that empathy plays a role in combating loneliness and mental health struggles. But now, the decision is ours to make. **Will we continue to overlook the transformative power of empathy, or will we choose to embrace it–not just for the sake of others but for our own emotional well-being, too?**

Building an Empathetic Tomorrow

"Empathy is the key to the future."

– Bill Drayton

If we truly want to create a world where empathy is the norm and loneliness becomes a thing of the past, we can't simply sit back and hope it happens naturally. We have to actively create it. Each of us has a role to play in shaping a tomorrow where compassion is the foundation, not just a reaction to hardship. This kind of change begins with something simple yet profound–listening. Not just with our ears but with our hearts. We often feel the urge to fix things, offer advice, and solve problems. But empathy isn't about problem-solving; it's about understanding and listening. A small act of listening costs you nothing, yet for the person whose world feels shattered, it can mean everything. It shows that you care, that you're willing to understand not just their story but the emotions behind it. Sometimes, the best way to show empathy is by just sitting with someone in their pain, letting them know that their feelings are valid and they are not alone. [16]

So, next time someone shares something with you, whether it's a victory, a struggle, or just a moment in their day, take a deep breath, pause, and listen with intention. And in doing so, we not only make the world more connected, but we also become more human ourselves.

To build an empathetic tomorrow, we must challenge ourselves to step outside our own perspective and truly see the world through someone else's eyes. It sounds simple enough, but it's far from easy. Consciously or unconsciously, we all have filters shaped by biases. These biases influence what we think and how we engage with the world around us. We must question the comfortable assumptions we carry daily, including those so ingrained that we barely notice them, the stereotypes that quietly shape our thoughts, and the prejudices that blur our ability to understand others.

Empathy demands that we reflect on our own biases before passing judgment. It asks us to pause and consider: what are we assuming about this person? Are we taking the time to truly understand their experiences, or are we simply fitting them into a narrative that feels comfortable to us? When we allow ourselves to set the assumptions aside, we create space where empathy can grow. The next time you encounter someone whose story or life experience is unfamiliar to you, look at them with fresh eyes, listen without judgment, and open your heart to their experience. The more we do this, the more we create a world where empathy is not just an occasional act but a natural, everyday part of how we connect with one another.

Empathy is indeed a fundamental human instinct. However, in a world where we're constantly scrolling through endless feeds, juggling deadlines, and racing to keep up with the hustle, it's easy to overlook. Before it becomes a lost art, we must recognise that empathy, like any other skill, can be developed and strengthened through practice.[17]

One way to restore the grip of empathy in our lives is through reading books.[18] I still remember the first time my father gifted me a book named *Chikku*. It was a children's storybook about a mouse who got separated from his mother. Lost and alone, he wandered through the world, facing countless struggles, fighting battles, and longing to reunite with his family. I read that story over and over again, each time feeling the young mouse's emotions more deeply–his fear, his sadness, his determination. I imagined what it must have felt like to be him, lost in a vast and unfamiliar world, yearning for the comfort of his mother's embrace.

I was only five years old then, but the story has stayed with me ever since. Through *Chikku*, I experienced emotions I had never fully understood before, all through the power of words. That little book was more than just a story. It was my first lesson in love, connection, and the magic of storytelling. Even now, whenever I think of *Chikku*, I remember not just the story but the warmth of the emotions. That's the power of a book in the world of empathy.

Through stories, we step into someone else's shoes, experience their joys and struggles, and understand emotions we might not have felt before. It's incredible how something so simple as reading can teach us to feel and care for others in ways we might not have expected. At the core, empathy involves the ability to understand and share the feelings of others. Reading, especially fiction, opens the doors to lives and experiences beyond our own. It also helps readers step into the shoes of characters from diverse backgrounds and historical contexts.

There are many books in my life that, from time to time, help me regain my grip on empathy. Each book turns into a doorway to a new perspective, helping me reconnect with the deeper human experiences. Charles Dickens's *Oliver Twist* draws me into the harsh world of a young orphan, highlighting society's neglect of the vulnerable and helping me connect with Oliver in a way that no statistic ever could. 'Americanah' by Chimamanda Ngozi Adichie offers a nuanced perspective on identity, immigration, and race through the lens of Ifemelu, a Nigerian woman trying to navigate life in America. Her journey of self-discovery and the struggles of fitting into new cultures make me reflect on my biases and assumptions.

Then there is *The Kite Runner* by Khaled Hosseini, a powerful tale of guilt, redemption, and the deep scars left by betrayal. I found myself deeply immersed in the complex relationship between Amir and Hassan, their bond of friendship shattered by secrets and choices that haunt them for years. The raw emotions of love, shame, and forgiveness resonated with me, pulling me into their world of deep struggles. Similarly, *The Vegetarian* by Han Kang offers an entirely different, yet equally poignant, exploration of personal conflict. It's a quiet, unsettling narrative about Yeong-hye, a woman who rejects societal expectations and retreats into her own world. Her decision to give up meat spirals into something far darker, demonstrating the power of choice and the unforeseen consequences that follow.

And then there is *Eleanor Oliphant Is Completely Fine*, where I meet Eleanor, a woman who lives in isolation, shaped by a painful past. Her quirky, socially awkward persona hides a deep emotional pain, and watching her open up to the possibility of connection gave me hope and comfort. Eleanor's healing journey made me realise how sometimes I need to take the first step toward my own emotional well-being, just as she did.

Through these books, I've walked alongside characters, experiencing their joys, sorrows, fears, and hopes. These moments of quiet reflection allow empathy to bloom again and again, deepening my understanding of others' lives. Unlike scrolling, which often involves skimming through fragmented content, reading encourages deep, uninterrupted engagement with a narrative. Yes, TV shows and movies can evoke empathy, but binge-watching can lead to passive consumption rather than active engagement. A book demands our full attention, pulling us away from the endless pings and scrolls of digital life.

So, instead of mindlessly scrolling through endless social media feeds or binge-watching yet another series, let's choose to pick up a book and reconnect with what truly makes us feel. Because the journey toward empathy often begins with a small yet powerful choice.

Before we can expect others to show us empathy or offer it to others, we need to first learn how to extend a fraction of it to ourselves. It's easy to get lost in the thoughts of "Why doesn't anyone understand?" or "Why does empathy feel like something I have to beg for?" These are the common thoughts that swirl when we're struggling with a lack of empathy. It often feels like we're trapped in a world that is deaf to the cries of those who need help the most.

But, loneliness doesn't only come from not receiving empathy from others. Sometimes, the deepest kind of loneliness comes from within when we struggle to offer empathy to ourselves. During my journey through depression, I spent so much time waiting for someone else to validate my pain, to tell me it was okay to feel the way I did. And when that didn't happen, I started blaming myself, shutting down, and pulling away from everyone. But why did I feel the need for someone else to validate my pain? What if I could be the one to offer myself the understanding I was desperately craving? What if I learned to listen to my own pain with kindness and empathy?

Brene Brown once said, "Talk to yourself like you would to someone you love." But for many of us, that kind of self-compassion doesn't come naturally, especially during a hard time. "I shouldn't feel this way," or "I'm not enough" - these internalised negative thoughts slowly erode our empathy for ourselves, replacing it with self-criticism and harsh judgment.

That's where the importance of self-empathy comes in. Self-empathy isn't some vague idea, it's about being kind and understanding toward our own emotions, acknowledging our struggles without judgment, and allowing ourselves the same compassion we would offer a friend.[19]Self empathy softens the inner dialogue. It helps quiet the shame. It allows space to feel without judgment. And slowly, it opens the door to healing–not just alone, but in connection with others.

When you fail an interview, don't jump to "I'm not good enough." Try saying instead, "It's okay. I gave it my best shot. Next time, I'll try again." When someone breaks your heart, don't fall into the trap of "I don't deserve love." Remind yourself, "I'm hurting right now, and that's valid. But I'll heal. The right person will come in time." When anxiety creeps in, resist the urge to label yourself as "weak." Say instead, "I'm feeling anxious right now, and that's okay. I can get through this."

That gentle, compassionate inner voice might feel unfamiliar at first. But over time, it begins to soften the harsh edges of self-judgment. It quiets the fear of what others might think–because the truth is, we often judge ourselves far more harshly than the world ever could. Self-empathy doesn't mean ignoring your pain. It means meeting it with kindness. And in doing that, we take a step toward breaking the cycle of loneliness. Because the more we learn to be there for ourselves, the more we're able to open up, connect, and let others in–without fear, without shame.

Every small act of kindness, whether toward ourselves or toward someone else, matters. Every choice we make shapes not just our own lives, but the world we leave behind. So the question is ours to answer: **Will we take empathy seriously? Will we make it the foundation of the world we want to build– a world where everyone feels seen, heard, valued, and, most importantly, less lonely, regardless of their background or circumstances?**

CHOICE 4

LOST IN NATURE VS LOST IN THE DIGITAL WORLD

"In nature, there is no loneliness. Even in solitude, the universe whispers its companionship."

– Leo Buscaglia

One of my fondest memories from childhood is spending winter breaks with my father at Kaziranga National Park. Every December, he would take me there, just an hour away from our home. But those trips were so much more than a simple get-away from school and exams. They were moments to bond with my father and make memories surrounded by the wild, untamed beauty of nature.

From the Latin names of plants to quiet life lessons, my father shared the wisdom of his fifteen years as a botanist with me in the most natural, effortless way. He had this way of making me see how nature quietly mirrors life, full of small connections and truths we often miss.

"Look," he once said, gently holding a Kopou Phool (foxtail orchid) in his hands. "This orchid is an epiphyte. It doesn't harm the tree it grows on; it simply uses it for support." He paused, looking at me with a thoughtful expression. "Life works the same way. It's okay to ask for help, but it's also important not to hurt others along the way."

I often wonder how he managed to find life lessons hidden in even the tiniest details of nature. Those conversations with him helped me see the world not just as a place to exist but as a living, breathing entity. Over time, I began to feel a sense of belonging there, as if the trees, the wind, the green around me were gently saying, "You're not lost, you're home."

After all this time, still, when life starts to feel too heavy, when the pace of modern life takes over, I know where to go. A walk through the woods, time by the river, or just lying under the open sky, nature has always been my escape, my reset button. It always feels like a space where I can breathe without the weight of everything else. But in those quiet moments, a thought sometimes lingers: Are those of us who feel most at peace in nature slowly being forgotten by a world that's too distracted to notice?

As American poet and essayist Gary Snyder once said, "Nature is not a place to visit. It is home".[1] However, over time, with each passing change, we have distanced ourselves from nature. The wildness has become an afterthought, a place to visit occasionally rather than a home that we are deeply connected to. Feeling a sense of belonging in the greenery seems like something out of a poet's notebook, an idea so rare it feels like it belongs to another time. We've started to take nature for granted, as if it's just a green screen to our busy lives. Everywhere I look, whether it's two-year-olds or seventy-year-olds, people are absorbed in the hypnotic glow of screens, allowing the true light of life to fade into the background. We search for solutions to our feelings of loneliness in endless scrolling, yet we never pause to consider that nature might hold the answers we're looking for.

"What is to blame for this?" I've been asked many times. Can we blame the relentless march of urbanisation, which has replaced fields, forests, and skies with concrete jungles that pull us further from nature? Or is it hustle culture pushing us to always do more, earn more, and chase something better? Or is it the portrayal of digital life as glamorous or essential, distracting us from the deeper, quieter world found in nature? The list of possibilities goes on and on.

Depending on our convenience, we can blame anything, but the truth is that our daily choices are the primary reason we've consistently sidelined nature, even as nature patiently waits for us to recognise and correct our mistakes. We, as a society, are responsible for creating generations disconnected from nature. Let's stop and think: Aren't we the ones allowing our children to stay glued to screens instead of encouraging them to explore the outdoors? Have we ever taken the time to educate anyone about the healing power of nature? Who is to blame when our actions are actually turning our cities into suffocating hubs of smog, haze, and pollution? Today, the Air Quality Index (AQI) in India's metro cities makes breathing in open spaces a daily challenge for several months each year.[2]

Urbanisation can certainly take its share of the blame, but if we look around, we can find numerous examples that prove urbanisation doesn't have to mean a disconnect from nature. A shining example is Singapore–a country that has become a global model for sustainable development. Known as the "Garden City," it has made green spaces a key part of its urban landscape. The city-state has transformed its urban areas by incorporating parks, green rooftops, and vertical gardens throughout the city. Iconic landmarks, Gardens by the Bay, a 101-hectare nature park that features futuristic Supertrees, biodomes, and themed gardens. The Supertrees, which range from 25 to 50 meters tall, are vertical gardens that house over 162,900 plants and serve as environmental engines for the gardens. Singapore Botanic Gardens are world-renowned examples of how nature can thrive alongside urban development.[3]

Costa Rica, known for its rich biodiversity, has successfully integrated nature into its economy and society despite facing challenges like poverty and rapid development.[4] South Korea also shows how technology and nature can coexist, finding balance amid fast urban growth. A clear example is the Cheonggyecheon Stream in Seoul, which was once buried under a highway for decades. Through the restoration project, the stream has been transformed into a vibrant, green public space that revitalises the area and attracts locals and tourists from around the world.[5]

In India, the city of Chandigarh stands as an example of how urban life and nature can coexist harmoniously. Chandigarh was planned by the renowned architect Le Corbusier and designed to be a "city of gardens," including extensive green belts, parks, and tree-lined avenues integrated into its urban planning.[6]

So it's not entirely fair to blame urbanisation for our growing disconnect from nature. The two don't have to cancel each other out. They can, in fact, grow side by side. All over the world, from cities in developed countries to fast-growing ones in developing nations, there are signs that nature can be invited back in. So it's not about whether urbanisation and nature can coexist. It's about whether we're ready to shift our mindset and truly value nature as an essential part of how we live.

Throughout history, the relationship between humans and nature has been one of both connection and disconnection. In ancient times, people lived in close rhythm with the earth; they hunted, gathered food from the land, and relied on natural signs to navigate life. Nature was a source of sustenance, wisdom, and comfort. But as civilisation progressed, urban growth and the pressures of modern life changed the way we relate to the natural world. Cities expanded, and with that expansion came a growing physical and emotional gap between people and the environment. We built walls–both literal and metaphorical–separating ourselves from the natural world, and as the hustle of life took over, the quiet presence of nature became something we only experienced in brief, disconnected moments.

Despite centuries of exploitation, pollution, and neglect, nature still has a remarkable way of calling us back. Forests still stand tall, their ancient roots reaching deep into the soil, supporting ecosystems and absorbing carbon. Rivers flow endlessly, carving their way through the landscape and sustaining life along their banks. The winds continue to whisper through the trees, carrying with them the essence of the natural world. Nature remains resilient and enduring, an ever-present force that continues to give.

Many of us still think of nature as just a giant, leafy air purifier that freshens the air. But that's a wildly limited view. Indigenous communities, ancient philosophers, and spiritual traditions across the world have long understood that the health of the earth is deeply tied to our own well-being. In India, for instance, nature is sacred. Traditional medicine like Ayurveda depends on the healing qualities of herbs, plants, and minerals. The River Ganga is worshipped as a goddess, and it is believed that the Hindu god Shiva resides in the Himalayas. Trees such as the Peepal and Banyan hold deep spiritual importance, valued not only for their role in the ecosystem but also for their sacred significance.[7]

And it's not just India. In ancient Greece, philosophers like Aristotle and Epicurus turned to nature to understand human existence, morality, and the pursuit of a good life.[8] They saw the natural world not as separate from humanity, but as a mirror–one that reflected our inner truths.

Modern science also continues to affirm the deep connection between nature and human health. People who spent time in green spaces said they felt less stressed and more relaxed. A study published in the journal *Frontiers in Psychology (2019)* found that spending at least 20-30 minutes in nature significantly lowers cortisol levels, a stress hormone.[9]Further research from the University of East Anglia (2018), which analysed data from over 140 studies, found that exposure to green spaces reduces heart rate, blood pressure, and other physiological markers of stress.[10] Another study published found that spending time in natural environments like parks or forests helped people feel less lonely and more connected to their communities.[11]

These evidences reinforce the idea that nature acts as a powerful antidote to the stressors of modern life. It can cut through the noise and overwhelm of daily life, giving our minds the breathing room they desperately need. Even without scientific studies, our own experiences also reflect this truth. Whenever we're stuck at work, we've all heard the familiar advice – "Go get some fresh air." And somehow, this advice always works. We've all experienced that quiet calm that washes over us the moment we step outside for a walk. The stress seems to lift, and our thoughts start to clear.

Nature has a unique way of resetting our minds, allowing us to return to a state of balance and clarity that is often hard to find in the chaos of daily routines. The birdsong, the sound of the river, and the texture of the grass always pull us back to the present. Not in a forced way but gently, like a friend taking your hand. One moment, you're lost in your head, replaying conversations or worrying about things you can't control, and then suddenly, you hear a river flowing beside you or catch the earthy scent of wildflowers –and just like that, you're here again. Nature doesn't ask you to figure anything out. It just offers itself–sound by sound, breath by breath–until the mental noise quiets down. The overthinking, the second-guessing, the pressure to be "okay", it all loosens its grip. What's left is something simpler. A moment. A breath. A sense of being where you are, not where your thoughts keep dragging you.

This is called "restorative attention," and it's one of the many healing gifts nature offers. Restorative attention is a form of focus that doesn't require active concentration.[12] When you're reading or working, your mind demands a lot of effort and energy. But when you're in nature, listening to the sound of birds or the flow of a river, restorative attention allows your mind to engage with the environment effortlessly. It's a gentle, passive connection that doesn't force you to think or concentrate. This effortless engagement offers your mind a much-needed mental break, giving you the space to reset and recharge without the pressure of active thought.

People who regularly engage in restorative experiences in nature report lower levels of anxiety, depression, and frustration. This emotional recovery not only fosters better mental health but also enhances overall happiness. In recent years, the practice of "forest bathing" or "Shinrin-yoku", a Japanese term that translates to "taking in the atmosphere of the forest", has gained significant attention as a therapeutic practice. This concept was developed in Japan in the 1980s as a response to the concerns over stress and mental health in urban populations.[13] Forest bathing is the practice of deeply connecting with the sights, sounds, smells, and textures of the forest. By focusing on the present moment and fully experiencing the environment, the mind is able to let go of stress and mental clutter. It helps shift attention away from the overwhelming demands of modern life, providing space for mental clarity and relaxation.

Nature also has a way of sparking deeper connections and encouraging meaningful conversations. I remember my father often telling me, "In these calm, peaceful surroundings, people tend to open up, sharing thoughts and feelings they might normally keep to themselves". He kept highlighting how nature creates a space for vulnerability and honest conversations. Honestly, I was just nodding along back then. But now, I truly understand every word he said.

For most of my life, I was guarded. I carried my emotions like delicate glass, always carefully tucked away, hidden behind walls even my closest friends couldn't quite reach. But in my marriage, I found a different kind of safety. I never had to fear expressing my emotions or sharing my thoughts. Surprisingly, that sense of safety began with our shared love for nature. In the early days, my husband and I made a simple promise to each other: no matter how busy life got, once a month, we'd step away and spend time in nature, just the two of us. It wasn't anything grand. A forest trail, a quiet lakeside, even a patch of green in the middle of the city.

In those moments, something shifted. We found more than just an escape in that rule; we discovered a space where we could truly see and hear each other. In that quiet, natural setting, I shared my thoughts on life, on love, on dreams, on everything that had once seemed too heavy to say aloud in a closed room. And in that exchange, we didn't just talk. We understood each other in a way that felt completely different from any other conversation. That's the power of nature.

Science backs it up, too. Group activities in natural settings, like hiking or forest walks, can significantly foster a sense of community and belonging. In the book "Your Brain on Nature", physician Eva Selhub and naturopath Alan Logan highlight something beautiful: Experiencing awe in nature, whether it's watching a sunset or standing before a vast mountain range, does more than inspire us. It brings us closer together. Experiencing these moments with others naturally brings people closer and deepens the connections we share.[14]

The list of ways nature supports us just keeps growing. From scientific research to everyday moments we all experience, the evidence is clear: nature plays a vital role in our well-being, both mentally and physically. Sometimes, I imagine that if nature were a person, she'd probably roll her eyes and say, "I've been your biggest cheerleader all along, but you've spent years tuning me out."

So, before it's too late, we need to make a choice: **Will we continue to turn a blind eye, or will we finally embrace the healing and connection we've been offering all along?**

Can Nature Bring Comfort in Loneliness?

"The more high-tech we become, the more nature we need."

– Richard Louv

Whenever loneliness knocks on my door and whispers, "You're not needed," "No one would miss you," or "It wouldn't matter if you were gone," I find myself pulled towards nature. Somehow, without saying a word, nature always knows how to hush that voice. It has always been that friend I didn't know I needed. It is the friend who offers a shoulder to rest on when I feel like the last person on Earth.

And, every time it happens, I find myself wondering, "Why does time in nature feel like a balm for my soul?"

Philosophically speaking, nature does not discriminate. It embraces all life, offering nourishment, shelter, and beauty without condition or expectation. A bird may sing to the sunrise, not for an audience or applause, but simply because the light brings life. The trees stretch their branches toward the sky, allowing their roots to intertwine with the earth, creating a community that supports one another in quiet cooperation. There is no performance. No need for validation. Rivers flow, nourishing everything in their path, knowing their journey will eventually return to the sea. They do it because they understand that each part of nature is a thread in the larger tapestry, and without each part, the whole would not thrive.

In all these quiet, generous acts, nature teaches us that compassion doesn't need to be earned or demanded–it exists in the very cycles of life, flowing freely for all to share. Maybe that's why, when we step into it, it feels like we've returned to a place that's always been waiting for us.

From a neurobiological perspective, being in nature activates the parasympathetic nervous system–the "rest-and-digest" response that helps us slow down, breathe deeper, and feel safe.[15] At the same time, it calms the sympathetic nervous system, which controls our fight-or-flight response. Edward O. Wilson, a renowned biologist and naturalist, explored this concept in his book *Biophilia* (1984), where he popularised the term "biophilia." Wilson proposed that humans have an innate, genetically ingrained affinity for the natural world. This instinct, he argued, is a result of evolution. Throughout history, our survival depended on understanding and interacting with nature, whether it meant finding shelter, locating food, or avoiding danger. Wilson's biophilia hypothesis suggests that humans are naturally wired to connect with nature and living things. That's why being around forests, rivers, or open landscapes brings us a deep sense of calm and renewal. [16]

The best part is that you don't even have to visit a forest or park to experience the magic of nature. It works its wonders in the simplest ways. Take sunlight, for instance. It is nature's multitasker. It is not just there to brighten our Instagram photos; it's essentially free mood therapy. It stimulates serotonin, a hormone that promotes feelings of happiness and well-being. This hormone slows the racing thoughts of loneliness and helps us to feel happy and calm at normal levels. Studies also say higher serotonin levels, induced by sunlight exposure, can improve attention span, problem-solving abilities, and promote mental clarity, which helps people engage more effectively in tasks and social settings.[17]

It's not just sunlight; every element of nature plays a role in nurturing our emotional well-being. But perhaps its most profound and unexpected gift is this: it reminds us that being alone doesn't have to mean being lonely. Nature has long been a muse. It sparks creativity, stirs deep emotions, and offers a canvas where the truest parts of the human spirit come alive. When we truly connect with nature, it starts to feel like the companion we've been searching for online but never found.

Since the dawn of humanity, artists, writers, and dreamers have long recognised this hidden gift of nature, turning to it as a wellspring of creative energy. Wordsworth found his poetry in the daffodils that danced in the breeze, Van Gogh poured the soul of the countryside into his wheat fields, and Thoreau, in his solitude at Walden Pond, unearthed the quiet wisdom and transformative power of nature. These are just a few examples of a long list of creators who have turned to nature, finding inspiration and healing in its beauty.

The way we see nature shapes what it becomes to us. John Muir, often called the "Father of the National Parks," once said, "In every walk with nature, one receives far more than he seeks". He forged a lifelong bond with nature that not only transformed his life but also allowed him to conquer the loneliness and alienation he often felt. Muri, born in Scotland in 1838 and raised in the United States, often felt out of place as a child. He was often restless, misunderstood, and out of sync with the world around him. But in the wild, he found what society could not give him: clarity, connection, and peace.[18]

Nature became his sanctuary, offering both solitude and clarity. In the stillness of the wilderness, Muir was able to process his inner strength and find peace away from the distractions of society. Through his writings and activism, Muir became a champion of the idea that nature could offer a refuge from modern life–a place for self-discovery, emotional processing, and spiritual rejuvenation. His time in the wild wasn't just about escaping the world; it was about learning to embrace the silence and stillness that nature provided, which allowed him to grow and evolve in ways that weren't possible within the constraints of everyday society.[19]

Muir's story reminds me that nature provides a space for emotional healing and self-realisation. His journey into the wilderness was an exploration of what it means to truly live, to feel at peace with oneself, and to connect with something greater than the individual. Brene Brown, a research professor at the University of Houston, has written extensively about the power of nature to ground us. She explains that nature can serve as a grounding force, offering solitude and space for reflection. These two things are vital when we face the emotional challenges of life, including loneliness.

In a world that constantly pulls us in a hundred directions, our overstimulated minds need a chance to breathe. To pause. To let go of all the noise. Perhaps it's time we stop seeing time spent in nature as a luxury and start viewing it as an opportunity to heal the loneliness within us. Perhaps it's time that instead of sitting alone at home thinking, "no one is with me," we stepped outside. Perhaps it's time we took a little moment to walk to the nearest park, to sit beneath a tree, to simply be.

Because believe me, in the company of nature, something shifts. Healing begins. Not loudly. Not all at once. But gently, like morning light creeping through the trees. Nature alone may not cure loneliness completely, but it can comfort it.

So next time the blanket of loneliness feels too heavy, make a choice: **Will you reach out to nature or slip into the trap of digital distraction, mistaking it for a cure to loneliness?**

Building Tomorrow that Embraces Nature

"In protecting nature, we protect ourselves and future generations."

– Rachel Carson

Today, saving nature is about more than just protecting the planet. It's about building stronger, more connected communities for the future. It's about fostering a life where our sense of grounding comes not from the strength of our internet signal but from the earth beneath our feet. Henry David Thoreau, the 19th-century American philosopher, naturalist, and writer, was one of the earliest thinkers to stress the importance of living closely with nature. Thoreau's influence on environmental thought, literature, and philosophy has been profound, especially through his experiences and writings.[20]

Thoreau spent two years, two months, and two days living in a small cabin near Walden Pond in Concord, Massachusetts. He immersed himself in nature to discover a life of deeper connection. For Thoreau, nature was a source of inspiration, wisdom, and spiritual renewal. He saw the natural world as a place where individuals could escape the distractions and materialism of society and reconnect with their inner selves. In his seminal work, *Walden*, Thoreau explains that he went to the woods to live deliberately and face only life's essential facts. His goal was clear: to strip away everything unnecessary, confront life in its rawest, most honest form, and search for meaning that went beyond the surface.[20]

He also warned of the dangers of losing touch with the natural world, criticising the hurried pace of society that distracts us from observing and appreciating nature's quiet rhythms. Thoreau felt that our constant chase for wealth and material things left us too drained to reconnect with nature or even with ourselves.

In today's world, his perspective feels not only relevant but essential. The disconnection he warned us about is now part of our daily routine. But so is the opportunity to return. If we hope to build a future that embraces nature rather than forgets it, then we must actively make conscious choices. Fortunately, many are already waking up to this truth. Across the world, people are planting trees, protecting forests, embracing sustainable fashion, reducing waste, and turning to renewable energy. We're learning, little by little, to tread more gently. Environmental movements are no longer just about saving the planet; they're about saving ourselves. They are about reconnecting with something real, something rooted, something that reminds us we belong.

But beyond that, we must also teach children how to build a meaningful connection with the natural world around them. An article published in *Times of India* mentioned that Generation Beta, encompassing individuals born from 2025 onwards, is poised to grow up in an era where technology and artificial intelligence are deeply integrated into daily life.[21] Without fostering a connection to nature, we risk raising a generation that feels alienated from its environment. The absence of this bond can leave deep emotional gaps, resulting in a profound sense of isolation later in life.

To rebuild the connection between children and nature, we should inspire them to truly observe nature, rather than simply watch it. There's a big difference between watching and observing. Watching might mean glancing at the trees while scrolling on a phone or noticing birds in passing. But observing goes deeper. It is active, mindful, and intentional. It means slowing down, engaging the senses, and getting curious. It's about asking questions, noticing details, and feeling connected to what's in front of you.

When children observe the shapes and patterns of leaves, the beautifully formed veins, and the varied colours, they open their minds to a world full of creativity, wonder, and connection. These simple moments of observation help them develop a deeper understanding of the elements of nature. They begin to slow down and savour the present moment. Watching a river twist and turn might lead them to ask, "How was it formed? Where does it go? What creatures call it home?" Suddenly, science and geography come alive with stories waiting to be uncovered.

These are the moments when children begin to develop a deeper connection with nature. But to make that bond lasting, we, as parents, educators, and mentors, must do more than speak about it. We must model it through our actions. That begins in the repeated moments when we choose to look up, step outside, and make space for the nature around us. For instance, instead of spending hours binge-watching TV shows or scrolling through screens, why not trade some of that time for an outdoor adventure? Whether it's hiking, cycling, or simply sitting quietly in the park, these small activities allow us to reconnect with the physical world and give our overactive minds the rest they need. If we can justify working through weekends in the name of productivity, then surely we can also make space for a quiet walk in the park, a moment beneath the trees, or time spent near a river. Tending to our well-being is just as essential as meeting deadlines.

It's time to recognise nature as a partner, not merely a resource to be used and overlooked. Governments are increasingly taking meaningful steps to reshape our cities by incorporating more trees, green rooftops, and accessible parks into urban planning.[22] These initiatives are more than just aesthetic improvements; they are investments in our health, well-being, and the sustainability of our communities. It's time for all of us to recognise and take full advantage of these positive changes. Supporting and expanding government efforts to integrate nature into our cities will not only enhance our quality of life but also ensure a healthier, more resilient planet for future generations.

Research from 2022 in *Scientific Reports* mentioned that individuals who spent at least 120 minutes weekly in natural settings experienced lower loneliness, even when social isolation was taken into account.[23] This is a powerful reminder that one of the simplest, most overlooked remedies for loneliness is right outside our door: nature. Even a brief walk can strengthen our connection to the environment, offering moments of peace and helping us appreciate the beauty of the world around us. So, why not? Why not let nature work its quiet magic on our hearts and minds?

Even small changes, like starting a garden, can have a profound impact on our lives. Whether it's in your backyard or on a balcony, gardening has been shown to reduce stress, improve mental well-being, and provide a real sense of accomplishment. There's something deeply fulfilling about caring for plants, watching them grow, and knowing you've had a hand in their development. Gardening gives us a chance to nurture something outside of ourselves, offering a pause from the chaos of daily life and helping us reconnect with the earth in a more meaningful way. In a world that often feels too fast and too disconnected, gardening creates a steady rhythm, grounding us in the present moment. In this simple act, we learn the value of patience, the joy of care, and the quiet rewards that come from nature's company.

How we interact with nature, how we teach the next generation to respect it, and how we prioritize time spent in the natural world will lay the foundation for the legacy we want to leave for generations to come. The most challenging aspect of building a future that truly embraces nature lies in a simple choice: **Are we ready to step outside and engage with the life-sustaining world around us?**

The answer to this question will define the relationship we, as individuals and as a society, have with nature in the years to come.

CHOICE 5

EMBRACE SOLITUDE VS FEAR SOLITUDE

"Silence is a source of great strength."

– Lao Tzu

I grew up in a nuclear family where both of my parents were always wrapped up in their work. Even though our family was small, our home was never really quiet. My mother was always on the go, moving between making meals and handling her responsibilities as the head of the school. Meanwhile, my father balanced his role as the head of a college while also actively contributing to local initiatives and projects that aimed to create meaningful changes in society. Politicians, educators, writers, and activists–every day, our home was filled with people from all walks of life. Some were there to consult with my mother about school matters, others seeking my father's insights on social issues.

Among these conversations, laughter, and visitors coming and going, I never truly felt a part of it. My role was simple: when guests arrived, I'd greet them with a Namaste and touch their feet for blessings. A few would show some interest in my life, but after a quick exchange, they also moved on to something else. As an introverted child, I also didn't have the ease to blend into the lively chaos around me. So, I created my own quiet space in my father's library where I could just be.

It wasn't just a room, it was my happy place. I could lose myself for hours there without ever feeling lost. I found joy in the shelves packed with stories, wisdom, and dreams. Whether it was an Assamese novel that chronicled the history of the Ahoms or a book on Vedic philosophy that sparked deeper questions about existence, I discovered a sense of companionship in those pages.

Was there really any pressure to fill the silence with sound? Not at all. I chose to see it as an opportunity to pause and listen to the subtle whispers of my own strength. I realised that this quiet nature wasn't a weakness–it was my foundation. I didn't need to chase after the noise or the chaos around me.

Was it loneliness? Not even close. It was peace. A glorious and uninterrupted peace. I never viewed spending most of my time alone as a struggle or a curse. It was simply the way I enjoyed it.

Was I always in "avoid people" mode? Absolutely not. I came alive in those moments with friends, revelling in the tiniest details, and conversations flowed effortlessly.

Enjoying my own company doesn't make me antisocial, and most importantly, being alone doesn't mean I am lonely. It simply meant I found comfort in solitude. But can today's world see it the same way? We often promote the belief that solitude is not a strength, but a weakness. The first thought when seeing a person sitting alone comes with an unspoken narrative: "Lonely?", "Sad?", "Awkward?" In the eyes of others, they're a puzzle to solve. We have started to believe that the absence of constant social interaction automatically equates to loneliness. The pressure to always be productive, to be seen, to stay engaged, and to constantly be 'on' makes solitude feel like something to be avoided.

From the moment we wake to the moment we sleep, not a single moment passes without some form of distraction pulling at our minds. When there's "nothing to do", people often turn to their phones. While travelling to work, we often listen to podcasts or scroll through social media. Because silence during commutes can feel monotonous or boring, distractions help pass the time. Even the simplest moments, like standing in a queue or waiting for an appointment, rarely go by without a quick check of Instagram or WhatsApp. Because waiting feels unproductive, and scrolling gives us a false sense of engagement or control. Many of us eat meals with a screen in front of us because entertainment makes the experience more stimulating.

Over time, filling the silence with distractions becomes a reflexive behaviour. I would agree that distractions can provide temporary comfort or entertainment, but they often prevent us from experiencing the benefits of silence. The need for external stimuli becomes such a part of our daily lives that moments of stillness feel almost like a foreign concept. Because of that, it gets harder and harder to enjoy the quiet and peace that come with being alone.[1]

Being alone is not something we can avoid. Sooner or later, we all encounter moments in life where we must stand alone. When we leave behind familiar places to chase our dreams in unfamiliar cities, there will be nights when we eat dinner alone, and the only footsteps echoing through the room will be our own. Parents who once built their world around their children are often left with quiet mornings and empty afternoons once their kids grow up. In a world that never slows down, where everyone is caught up in their lives, it's not unusual to find ourselves alone, especially during the tougher chapters of life. And, when someone we love–a parent, a partner, a close friend–is no longer in this world, they leave behind more than just silence. They leave behind an emptiness that's hard to describe.

So maybe the question isn't how we escape being alone, but how we learn to transform this aloneness into the power of solitude rather than loneliness. If we believe that relying heavily on digital media can truly answer our question, then perhaps we are missing the point. Because if that were the case, why is it that 65% of Gen Z, the most digitally connected generation, still fighting with loneliness?[2]

There's nothing inherently wrong with turning to digital media for a bit of distraction, or even for comfort when we feel alone. Sometimes, a funny video from a friend or a quick message from a stranger really can brighten a heavy moment. But the problem begins when we start fearing solitude, treat solitude like something to be avoided, and use digital noise as a shield. Over time, this constant avoidance becomes a habit, and these habits make us more emotionally fragile. We forget that solitude isn't the same as loneliness. It's not something to fear–it's actually what helps us reconnect with ourselves in ways all the noise and distractions never could.

The basic difference between solitude and loneliness is that solitude is about enjoying being alone, while loneliness is about struggling with being alone. In solitude, you choose to be alone. It's your choice to sit alone with a cup of coffee, no notifications, just your thoughts, and somehow you feel complete in that quiet. Solitude is like giving your mind a chance to breathe and start fresh. Loneliness, on the other hand, isn't something you choose. It sneaks in even when you are surrounded by people. Loneliness is not the absence of people. It is about the absence of connection. Solitude is a gift. But loneliness feels like a punishment.[3]

People embrace solitude for self-reflection. Writers, artists, and musicians often seek solitude to unlock their creative potential, proving that some of the greatest ideas are born in solitude. A walk in nature or practising mindfulness alone can calm the mind, ease anxiety, and strengthen emotional resilience. On the other hand, prolonged loneliness can lead to depression, anxiety, low self-esteem and many more.[4]

I won't deny that loneliness and solitude share common ground. Both involve physical separation from others and leave us alone with our thoughts. "What now?", "Why is no one around me?" These questions creep in, whether we are in loneliness or in the early stages of embracing solitude. And it's very easy to slip from one into the other. The discomfort, the subtle ache of being alone, can convince us that we are missing out on the joy of human connection, that being alone means being left behind.

But still, no matter how narrow the line between loneliness and solitude may appear, it's a distinction worth understanding. Especially today, when the experience of being alone is no longer rare, but an inevitable part of life. In a world where more people live independently and spend less time in the presence of genuine relationships, it's important that we learn to embrace solitude rather than fear it. If we keep filling our moments of solitude with distractions, we may face a future where algorithms shape all our beliefs and choices, leading us to lose our authenticity in a sea of noise. Solitude is no longer just a poetic ideal; it is a way to reflect, reset, and reclaim control over our thoughts and emotions before we become puppets of the digital world.

Science shows that our brain's default mode network becomes active when we step away from the noise. This network is responsible for deep self-reflection. It turns solitude into a space for emotional growth and self-awareness. So instead of feeling isolated or disconnected, we find clarity in these quiet moments.[5] Research has also found that solitary activities like meditation, journaling, or just quiet reflection can significantly reduce cortisol, the primary stress hormone. When the mind is free from the constant pressures of digital overstimulation, it gets much-needed space to breathe and recharge. This mental reset doesn't just help manage stress–it enhances focus, promotes recovery, and improves overall well-being, both mentally and physically.[6]

Steve Jobs, co-founder of Apple, often spent time alone to reflect and clear his mind. He believed solitude was essential for gaining clarity and perspective. His habit of taking long walks alone helped him focus on the details and fueled his creativity. Many groundbreaking ideas that shaped Apple's products were born in those moments of solitude.[7]

Haruki Murakami, the internationally acclaimed novelist, spends much of his time in solitude. He adheres to a disciplined routine of running, writing, and reflecting. Murakami's ability to immerse himself in his inner world has led to bestselling novels like *Kafka on the Shore* and *Norwegian Wood*, which resonate deeply with themes of isolation and introspection.[8]

Swami Vivekananda often spent time in quiet places to meditate and reflect. These moments of stillness helped him find the clarity that shaped his teachings on spirituality and self-awareness.[9] The poet Rainer Maria Rilke also believed that solitude was key to creativity and truly knowing oneself. In *Letters to a Young Poet*, he emphasises how important it is to be alone to understand who you really are.[10] Albert Einstein also valued solitude, using it as a space for deep thinking and creativity. Many of his groundbreaking theories were born from quiet reflection.[11]

Throughout history, those who truly embraced solitude never mistook it for loneliness. They didn't see being alone as a sign that they were unloved or unworthy. They didn't run from the quiet, fearing they were missing out on life. They became who they were because they understood something most of us forget: solitude can be a gift. Whether it was Steve Jobs, Swami Vivekananda, Haruki Murakami, Rainer Maria Rilke, or Albert Einstein, all were visionaries, leaders, and architects of thought who helped shape the course of culture and history. But let's be clear–they weren't antisocial, nor were they lonely. They didn't choose solitude because they disliked people; they chose it because they understood its purpose.

Now the choice is ours: **Do we still see solitude as a curse, or do we want to discover what it's been trying to show us all along?**

Significance of Solitude in Various Cultural Practices

"The quieter you become,
the more you are able to hear."

– Rumi

Our relationship with solitude may have shifted with time, but the connection itself is ancient. If we look back, many cultures not only embraced solitude, but they also revered it. Let's take Hinduism, for instance, one of the world's oldest spiritual traditions, with roots reaching as far back as 1500 BCE. In its teachings, solitude isn't just about spending time alone. It's about stepping into a space of sacred silence where the noise of the world fades away, allowing one to connect directly with the divine essence.[12]

Sadhana, a Hindu spiritual practice, is an intimate, quiet path of discipline and devotion. Whether it's meditation, chanting, prayer, or deep self-inquiry, the essence of sadhana is about stepping away from the noise, not permanently, but long enough to hear what's unfolding inside. Ancient Hindu scriptures, such as the Upanishads, teach that the ultimate truth, Brahman, goes beyond words and sound. It can only be truly known through direct experience in solitude.[13]

The Bhagavad Gita, one of the most ancient religious scriptures, teaches that true insight emerges when one steps away from the noise and distractions of the world.

"योगीयुञ्जीतसततमात्मानंरहसिस्थितः |
एकाकीयतचित्तात्मानिराशीःअपरिग्रहः ||"

(Bhagavad Gita, 6.10)

(Yogi yunjita satatam atmanam rahasi sthitah
Ekaki yatacittatma nirasih aparigrahah)

Translation:

"Let the yogi always try to concentrate his mind by remaining in solitude, living alone, with controlled mind and body, free from desires and possessions."

In this verse of the Bhagavad Gita, the true yogi is described as one who seeks solitude (*rahasi sthitah*) not as an escape, but as a sacred setting for inner alignment. The practice of yoga here is not just physical; it is a journey inward. The yogi disciplines both mind and self (*yatacittātmā*), understanding that real clarity comes not from the noise of the world, but from the quiet strength within.[14]

Hindu practices place great emphasis on solitude as a path to inner peace, a way to tune into the inner wisdom, and a means to experience unity with the divine. Similarly, in Buddhism, solitude is seen as a path to clarity, wisdom, and liberation. The journey unfolds through three meaningful stages.

The first stage is Physical Solitude (Kāya-viveka)–an outer stillness that opens space to reconnect with your inner self. The image of the Buddha sitting quietly beneath the Bodhi tree shows us the profound power of silence on the path to awakening. A monk walking alone at dawn or sitting peacefully by a mountain stream teaches us to choose calm over chaos. This stage of solitude isn't about escaping the world–it's about coming home to yourself.

Next comes Mental Solitude (Citta-viveka). Even when everything around us is quiet, the mind can still be noisy. This stage of solitude is about letting go of that inner clutter–the constant swirl of thoughts, desires, worries, and stories. It's about learning to sit with whatever arises, and watching those thoughts drift by like clouds in the sky. Finally, there's Ultimate Solitude (Upadhi-viveka)–the deepest and most profound kind of solitude. It goes beyond simply stepping away from the world or quieting the mind. In this solitude, there is no "I" to defend, no identity to uphold, no desire to chase. Just pure, luminous awareness–still, open, free. This is the solitude of Nirvana. It isn't emptiness in the way we often fear. It is liberation.[15]

Each stage of solitude isn't something to rush toward or force, but something we grow into over time.Those who practice solitude begin to see the core teachings the Buddha shared: the impermanence of all things (anicca), the inherent dissatisfaction in clinging to them (dukkha), and the absence of a fixed, separate self (anatta). With these insights, solitude becomes a foundation for walking the Eightfold Path–especially supporting Right Effort, Right Mindfulness, and Right Concentration.[15]

Beyond religious practices, countries like South Korea and Japan have cultivated unique ways to embrace solitude, not as loneliness, but as a meaningful practice to recharge, reflect, and find balance. In Japanese culture, solitude is deeply intertwined with Zen Buddhism. Solitary meditation invites stillness and self-awareness in Zen teachings. The beauty of emptiness is also celebrated in Japanese art, architecture, and music. Take Kintsugi, for example, the art of repairing broken pottery, done in quiet solitude, honouring imperfections rather than hiding them. And then there's Shinrin-yoku, or "forest bathing," where solitary walks in nature help clear the mind and restore balance.[16]

Much like Japanese Zen, Korean Seon Buddhism places deep importance on silence and solitude as sacred steps along the path to enlightenment. In the quiet spaces–often high in the mountains or deep within forest hermitages–monks retreat from the world not to escape it, but to see it more clearly. But solitude in Korea isn't just a monastic tradition; it's also finding new life in the modern world. In today's South Korea, a growing cultural movement known as Honjok– the "Alone Tribe"–has redefined solitude as something empowering rather than shameful. These are people who live, eat, and explore life on their own terms–not from isolation, but from intention.[17]

This cultural shift has even given rise to a new language that honours the joy of doing things alone. Honbap, eating alone, was once considered uncomfortable or even embarrassing, but now it's embraced as a chance to enjoy a meal fully, without distraction. Honsul, the act of drinking alone, has become a gentle form of self-care, a time to unwind at your own pace. And Honnol, or playing alone, whether it's travelling solo, going to a movie, or immersing yourself in a personal hobby, celebrates the simple freedom of being content in your own company. No performance, no justification–just you, fully present in the moment.[17]

Solitude has also long held a place in the Korean literary soul. In classic Korean poetry, such as Yun Seon-do's *The Fisherman's Calendar*, frames solitude as a way to connect with nature. It's not about being alone for the sake of being alone. It's about finding peace and harmony in that solitude. It's about stepping away from the chaos of life and letting the natural world speak to you.[18]

Similarly, in Western cultures, solitude is often associated with independence, self-reflection, and personal growth. It is seen as a way to recharge, find creativity, or achieve mindfulness. In Nordic cultures, such as Sweden and Norway, solitude is often valued as a personal space for quiet reflection. It is seen as a natural and respected part of life. Concepts like Hygge(cosiness) in Denmark or Friluftsliv (open-air living) in Norway emphasise the balance between social connection and the solitary enjoyment of nature. [19]

Across cultures, shaped by history, spirituality, and societal influences, solitude is never portrayed as something to fear. Whether in Hinduism, Buddhism, Japan, South Korea, or Norway, solitude holds the potential for some of the most transformative personal growth experiences. Rather than being a source of fear, it is seen as a powerful opportunity for clarity and inner peace. There is no doubt that when we intentionally seek solitude, we can overcome the pain of loneliness and nurture a deeper, more authentic connection with ourselves.

But the question remains: **Will we give ourselves the space to truly embrace the power of solitude, or will we keep letting fear hold us back?**

Why Does Solitude Scare Us Today?

***"If you are lonely when you are alone,
you are in bad company."***

– Jean Paul Sartre

From a young age, we're taught, explicitly or not, that connection equals safety. We are wired to believe that being with others means we are protected. We are told to get married because "you can't be alone." We are told to have children so "you won't be alone when you're old". We dive into social media in the search for connections, even though we know it's addictive and the connections are superficial, because we are afraid of what might surface in silence. Introverts are taught to mimic extroverts, not because they want to, but because deep down, they believe that if they don't socialise enough, they'll eventually spiral into loneliness. We treat solitude like quicksand: something to escape from as fast as possible.

The reason behind this isn't just cultural, it's also biological.

Back in our evolutionary days, being alone did mean danger. It made it harder to find food and easier to be attacked. Connection wasn't just comforting; it was crucial for survival. Our brains adapted to associate closeness with safety, to read isolation as a red flag. Even after thousands of years, though the external world has changed, our homes have locks and our kitchens are full, our internal wiring remains the same.

That's why solitude can still feel unsettling, even when there's no immediate danger. The amygdala, our brain's fear centre, doesn't differentiate between a predator lurking in the dark and the silence of an empty apartment. It registers the absence of social cues as a potential threat, and in response, it goes on high alert. Thoughts begin to spiral, and anxiety creeps in without warning. We feel restless, uneasy and unsure. The quiet, which should feel peaceful, instead is charged with discomfort.[20]

This is part of being human. It's why, for almost everyone, solitude at first feels uncomfortable, even scary. That uneasy feeling is simply old wiring, outdated survival mechanisms doing their job, trying to protect us from dangers that no longer exist in the same way. Our minds may still react to quiet moments with caution, interpreting the lack of stimulation as something to be fixed. But in truth, the world around us has changed. We are not in immediate danger when we sit alone in a quiet room. We are not at risk when walking alone through a park or sitting silently.

Another reason solitude feels scary for many in today's generation is that it forces us to sit with our own thoughts. And that's what frightens us the most. We are not just alone in a room; we are alone with unfiltered, unedited, raw thoughts. We were taught how to succeed, how to socialise, how to stay busy, but not how to sit quietly with our thoughts without distractions.We have gotten used to filling every quiet moment with something, anything, that drowns out the stillness.

So, when that noise fades and we are left with silence, all the buried thoughts rise to the surface. The negative ones - the fears, the doubts, the insecurities - unfold. The unresolved emotions we've pushed aside reappear. Even the positive thoughts– the desires, the dreams, the truths about who we really are and what we truly want– can feel overwhelming, simply because they're honest. A few moments of silence can strip away our masks and hold up a mirror to the parts of ourselves we've been too busy or too scared to face. We've become so used to playing roles and keeping busy that the company of our own selves has, ironically, become the scariest place to be.

But this discomfort isn't a reason to run from solitude; it's a call to lean into it. Instead of seeing it as a warning, we should recognise it as a chance to acknowledge and understand our thoughts. Rather than drowning them out with distractions, we can learn to sit with them, which helps us grow and find clarity.

Another reason solitude feels unsettling is that we crave an audience for everything. We want to be seen and heard because somewhere deep inside, we've tied our sense of existence to that validation. We think, "If someone responds to me, then I exist". But in solitude, there is no audience. No likes, no comments, no affirming nods. Just us. So for many, that absence feels like erasure. The fear of being forgotten, of going unnoticed, is so strong that we're afraid of even a few moments of solitude. It makes us avoid silence and seek constant connection, just to remind ourselves that we matter.[21]

Social media has turned this fear into a weapon, making solitude feel like failure. But here's the truth: the need for an audience is deeply human, yet it can also trap us. If we live only to be seen, we become actors in our own lives, always performing, never quite living. Solitude invites us to step away from the spotlight, to strip off the layers of performance, and to sit with ourselves, not as personas, but as real, living people. But before we can experience solitude as sanctuary, we must make a choice: **Are we ready to embrace solitude or are we still afraid of it?**

That choice is everything. It becomes the bridge between solitude as peace and solitude as a curse.

Embracing Solitude

"I find solitude is the best way to discover my inner self."

– David Gilmour

Embracing solitude may sound simple in theory, but in reality, it often feels like swimming against the current, especially in a world where slowing down can be mistaken for falling behind. For years, I was caught in the relentless chaos of the IT world– deadlines, back-to-back meetings, and constant demands. Every moment buzzed with noise. Even when I wasn't working, I was either at a party or wrapped up in my social life.

It felt like I was constantly moving, chasing the next task, the next goal, the next "important" thing. Life became a room with no windows, no space to breathe, no time to pause. Any rare moment of solitude felt wrong, like a glitch in the system. I did everything I could to fill that silence. Simple moments, like just talking to myself in the mirror, were replaced by a podcast playing in the background. Because I believed learning never really stops. There's always something new to learn, something to stay updated on. And the short breaks between meetings? They got consumed by mindless scrolling–endlessly flicking through content, convinced that I might miss some crucial trend, or worse, some breaking news that I was supposed to know.

But I never felt fulfilled. There was a growing emptiness that lived right in the middle of the chaos.

"Am I missing something?"

"Am I being productive enough?"

The more I asked, the more anxious I became. The quiet I once enjoyed in my father's library as a child had vanished in the rush. But in 2024, something inside me cracked. I could feel it deep in my bones–a quiet, insistent need for something different. Maybe a reset. So, I did what terrified me the most: I quit my job for a year and moved to South Korea with my husband.

When I arrived in South Korea, I had no idea what the future held - no plan, no roadmap. In fact, I didn't speak the language, one spoken by over 90% of the people around me. My husband was soon swept up in his office work, and the time difference with my home country made it hard to stay connected with friends and family. My days, once filled with endless meetings and buzzing emails, suddenly stretched into long silences. At first, the stillness felt almost unbearable. I had been so conditioned to thrive in the rush, the chaos, and the demands of my past life that this sudden emptiness felt almost threatening.

But now looking back, I realised that discomfort was something I needed. Maybe, in fact, it was exactly what I had been striving for all along. As the days passed, I started to embrace that silence.

I took a digital detox, something I had never imagined myself doing, and the world slowed down. In the stillness, I began to turn inward. I found myself confronting one question I had long buried beneath the noise of everyday life.

"What do I really want to do in my life?"

The question was simple, but for the first time, I didn't run from it with distractions. Instead, I paused, sat with it, and made space to uncover the answers. And then, like a flood, inspiration began to flow. My passion for writing, a hobby I had once brushed aside, surged back to life. Ideas for my first book came to me in waves, each one more fluid and effortless than the last. I understood what it meant to truly hear my own voice, to listen to myself without the world's constant chatter drowning me out. I realised that when we embrace solitude, we open ourselves up to a deeper connection with our emotions.

One of the most powerful ways to embrace solitude is to treat it as an invitation for self-discovery and deep reflection.[22] In the quiet moments alone, we can ask ourselves, "What am I truly working towards?", "What brings me joy–not just fleeting happiness, but deep, lasting fulfilment?" or "What fears hold me back from reaching my potential?" These questions may sound like they belong in a philosophical book, but this kind of soul-searching can help us in ways we never imagined. In these moments, solitude becomes a space to listen for honest and unfiltered answers.

Another powerful way to embrace solitude is to use it as a space where your creativity can flow freely and your ideas can take shape without interruption.[22] When we paint, write, cook, or compose music in solitude–just for the joy of it–we shift our focus from outcome to process. There's freedom in that. These moments of pure self-expression help us reconnect with our inner voice, which doesn't need validation. In solitude, creativity becomes less about performance and more about exploration.

Social media often sends the message that we should always be sharing, reacting, and performing, as if our worth depends on our visibility. But to truly embrace solitude, we must learn to set boundaries with the digital world. Start by reminding yourself: "This is my time to recharge, not perform." Create tech-free hours in your day–little windows where your attention belongs fully to you. Try a digital detox, even just for a day, and notice how your mind begins to settle and how your inner voice grows louder without the constant scroll. Even if it feels uncomfortable at first, stepping away from the routine you've grown used to is essential.

Embracing solitude is like any journey of self-improvement–it takes time and practice. If it feels hard at first, don't worry. Start small and be patient with yourself. Try this: sit by a window without any plans or distractions. Let some music play softly–not to change how you feel, but just to be there with you. Let the moment be slow and intentional. Make it your own. Or, you could begin or end your day with a little quiet time, maybe by journaling. Don't worry about grammar or making it perfect–just write whatever comes to mind. This kind of journaling helps you express what's inside and lets you observe your feelings instead of getting caught up in them.

What really matters isn't the activity itself, but the intention behind it–to spend time with yourself, not feeling lonely, but feeling calm and connected. As you continue on that path, you'll begin to crave them more, seeing them not as a gap in your day but as a necessary space to reconnect with your inner self, reflect, and create. Even after giving it a try, if solitude still feels uncomfortable, take a moment to pause and ask yourself: "What am I avoiding by staying busy?" The answer might be the truth you've been needing to hear.

I've never said that embracing solitude means cutting ourselves off from the world or sitting alone in a quiet room all day. It simply means making space to be with our own thoughts, without constantly chasing what everyone else is doing. Always keep in mind that Solitude isn't about disconnection. It's not something to fear. It's about reconnecting with a kind of peace that doesn't need an audience. While it's true that too much solitude can slip into isolation, intentional alone time–when used for reflection rather than escape–can actually deepen our ability to connect more authentically with others. As philosopher Paul Tillich wrote, "Loneliness expresses the pain of being alone, while solitude expresses the glory of being alone."

Choosing solitude in today's fast-paced world can feel like a quiet act of rebellion. But it's not impossible–it just begins with intention. If you truly want it, there are a thousand ways to welcome it in. But if you're running from it, you'll find a thousand excuses too. Too busy, too tired, too connected to disconnect. The problem isn't in the availability of time; it's in the willingness to pause.

So, before the day slips away, ask yourself again: **Will you choose to welcome solitude with intention and not as something to fear or keep filling the silence with distractions?**

CHOICE 6

EASING LONELINESS WITH TECH VS ESCALATING IT

> ***"Loneliness is not a function of solitude. Loneliness is a function of how socially adept you are at adapting to solitude."***
>
> **– David Foster Wallace**

A girl sits alone in her room, her dinner growing cold on the plate as she immerses herself in a conversation in the metaverse. The conversation feels so real, so vivid, that she can almost sense the presence of her digital companion sitting beside her. In the room next door, her brother dines alone while recording himself for his vlog. He talks animatedly about his diet and what's on his plate, describing each bite with practised ease. His voice flows with enthusiasm, every word carefully crafted for the thousands of viewers who will engage with him through likes, comments, and shares. It seems as if he's connected to people all around the world, yet the only company in the room is his own reflection in the camera lens.

This isn't a snapshot from a sci-fi movie; it's a haunting truth of tomorrow where we're endlessly connected to distant voices, yet strangely disconnected from the person sitting just across the room. One escapes into the metaverse, chasing stimulation in virtual worlds. The other curates moments for strangers online, performing for likes and validation. It's strange, isn't it? The very technology that promised to bring us closer is slowly turning the people under our own roof into strangers.

Back in 2011, Apple introduced Siri with the iPhone 4s, bringing the first taste of AI into millions of hands. A simple voice command could set a reminder or answer a question, marking the start of AI becoming part of our daily rhythm. Fast forward to 2014, Amazon took the next step with Alexa, a voice-powered assistant paired with the Echo speaker. With its ability to control smart homes and handle everything from setting timers to answering questions, Alexa made AI even more accessible, turning homes into interactive spaces. But the real revolution didn't come until November 2022, when OpenAI launched ChatGPT. This wasn't just another assistant – it could generate human-like text, write essays, hold conversations, and tackle tasks in ways that felt almost magical.

This breakthrough ignited the rise of generative AI tools like DALL-E, MidJourney, and Stable Diffusion, unlocking the ability for users to craft art, music, and content with nothing more than a few simple prompts. Tech giants like Google, Microsoft, and Meta put billions into integrating AI into everything from search engines to social media. It wasn't just a tool anymore; it was quickly becoming part of how we create, communicate, and connect.[1]

But is that all AI amounts to? Far from it. AI has stepped into the role of a companion. It can simulate empathy, actively listen, and respond in ways that make users feel heard and understood. In a world full of complex human interactions, AI offers a simpler kind of connection. It creates a non-judgmental space where users can share their thoughts, fears, or struggles without the worry of being misunderstood or judged. In this way, AI provides comfort and connection to those who feel isolated.

Let's take a closer look at some examples. Replika, created by Eugenia Kuyda, is an AI chatbot designed to give personal companionship and emotional support.[2] Essentially, it provides users with a personalised AI friend. Another example is Woebot, an AI-driven mental health chatbot that applies Cognitive Behavioural Therapy (CBT) techniques to assist users in managing their emotions.[3] It provides a judgment-free space where users can express their feelings and get immediate, supportive feedback, available 24/7. Similarly, Wysa, created by Jo Aggarwal, combines chatbot conversations with evidence-based therapeutic techniques to help individuals improve their emotional well-being.[4] These tools are reshaping the way we approach mental health and human connection, offering a layer of support that's always accessible. Isn't it remarkable or maybe even a little surreal to see how technology is now fulfilling the emotional roles we once relied on friends, family, or others to provide?

Japanese company GROOVE X introduced an AI-powered robot, Lovot, in December 2018, with the goal of bringing joy and emotional comfort. Lovot redefines companionship by acting less like a machine and more like a loving, living being.[5] It doesn't just "see" its user, it strives to "feel" them emotionally with the help of an advanced algorithm. With lifelike behaviours, it responds to touch, recognises its owner, and remembers past interactions. Unlike Siri's functional responses or Alexa's monotone reminders, Lovot is designed to foster a genuine bond. This cuddly companion offers unconditional affection, creating a safe space where individuals can express their truest selves without fear of judgment.

The allure of AI companions, like Lovot, is undeniable, especially in an era where loneliness has become a public health crisis. Studies found that participants who interacted with AI companions reported feeling less lonely and experiencing a greater sense of companionship.[6] But let's pause for a moment. While AI assistants or virtual realities may help alleviate the pain of loneliness, what happens when future generations grow up seeking comfort from robots rather than parents, siblings, or friends?

Every day, brilliant minds are working tirelessly to create innovations that are redefining reality, bringing to life experiences we could only dream of a decade ago. From casual chats to deeper, more meaningful conversations, these technologies are offering a level of convenience, empathy, and understanding that was once the domain of human relationships. In fact, studies reveal that one in four young adults around the world believe AI could one day replace real-life romantic relationships.[7]

The Replika AI Chatbot app allows users to create a customisable virtual friend or romantic partner that learns from conversations over time. It can offer emotional support, engage in deep discussions, and even participate in role-playing scenarios. Similarly, AI girlfriend app Anima allows users to chat, flirt, and build virtual relationships, blurring the line between genuine connection and simulation, raising important questions about what companionship truly means in the digital age.

Not only AI, today Extended Reality (XR), which includes VR, AR, and MR, isn't just changing how we communicate; it's fundamentally reshaping the way we connect as humans. In the metaverse, the boundaries of geography and time are rapidly vanishing. Meta (formerly Facebook) has also developed tools for businesses to conduct operations in the metaverse, including Horizon Workrooms.[8] This platform is designed to facilitate virtual meetings, allowing teams to collaborate in immersive environments that feel more like a physical office setting, despite being fully digital. Microsoft has also made strides with its Mesh for Microsoft Teams product, integrating mixed-reality experiences into its popular collaboration platform.[9] Companies are shaping the future of work by creating virtual environments that make traditional in-person business activities more accessible, interactive, and engaging, transcending physical limitations.

In 2024, Apple's Vision Pro, a mixed reality headset, is set to redefine immersive experiences. This device, designed for seamless integration with Apple's ecosystem, features groundbreaking technologies like EyeSight and Optic ID, which promise to create more intuitive and personalised user interactions. Whether it's attending virtual meetings, exploring new entertainment avenues in digital worlds, or simply engaging in real-time collaboration, technology promises to bring people closer in ways that go beyond traditional screens.[10]

It's tempting to think that technology can give us the connection and understanding we've been craving in human relationships.

But at the same time, it's hard not to feel a bit scared about what happens when these artificial connections start replacing the real, messy, imperfect bonds we have with each other. Human beings are special because they express love through sacrifice, vulnerability, and mutual growth. These qualities evolve and deepen over time as people navigate life together. Yet, AI companions are beginning to mimic this real love, using Natural Language Processing (NLP) to understand our words, engage in meaningful conversations, and adapt their responses to feel more human-like than ever.[11] With technology, we are creating a new form of intimacy–one that transcends physical proximity, but the question is: Will this version of intimacy truly satisfy the deep, human longing for authenticity? The answer to that question may shape the future of the loneliness epidemic. Maybe, without realising it, we've started giving up the messiness and imperfection of human relationships for something easier, something convenient. But will "convenience" ever be enough to make us feel seen?

Satya Nadella, the CEO of Microsoft, has always been a strong advocate for the positive potential of artificial intelligence (AI), especially when it comes to addressing issues like loneliness and improving human connection. For him, AI isn't just about advancing technology for business; it's about using it to bridge societal divides, create opportunities for personal growth, and provide support to those feeling isolated. He's a firm believer in the idea of "AI for Good," advocating for AI that benefits people and society as a whole.[12] However, at the same time, philosophers and authors Yuval Noah Harari offer a more cautious perspective. Harari suggests that AI-driven virtual companions or chatbots could become substitutes for human relationships, especially for those who struggle with loneliness. While he acknowledges the potential of AI to offer comfort and connection, he also questions whether these artificial relationships can ever provide the same depth, authenticity, or emotional richness as human connections. According to Harari, while AI might fulfill some emotional needs, it can't replicate the complexities and genuine empathy that come from real human interaction. This opens up a larger conversation about the role of technology in human relationships, whether it enhances our lives or risks replacing the very essence of connection we need.[13]

The debate around whether AI-driven convenience can truly fill the void of loneliness is far from settled, and maybe it never will be. But one thing is certain: loneliness isn't what it used to be. For generations before us, loneliness simply meant the absence of people around you –quiet moments in an empty room, days without company, or long distances between loved ones. But somewhere along the way, the definition began to shift. Today, loneliness is more about feeling emotionally invisible. It can be found in the middle of crowded cafes, buzzing group chats, or family dinners where no one looks up from their screens. It is present in relationships where two people sleep in the same bed, but live in entirely different emotional worlds.

Because the nature of loneliness has changed, maybe the solution must evolve too. Perhaps it's not just about more interaction, but more real interaction. In this digital illusion, it's easy to forget that no AI, no metaverse, no

beautifully designed chatbot can replace the warmth of a hug or the quiet comfort of someone simply sitting beside you in silence.

A screen might reply with perfect timing, say all the right words, even mimic empathy, but it will never truly feel you. Maybe talking to an AI chatbot is easier than booking a ticket, taking time off work, and showing up for a tough conversation with someone you love. But emotional shortcuts rarely lead to genuine connection.

So every time you choose the easy way out, take a pause and ask yourself: **Is this new form of connection truly making it easier for us to feel connected? Or is it quietly pulling us away from the real world?**

VR and MR: A Friend or A Foe to Loneliness

"We are becoming more and more isolated, and technology is making it worse."

– Jaron Lanier

Before VR, gaming was mostly confined to PCs or in-person meetups with friends. It required planning, interaction, and being physically present. Similarly, exploring new places meant actually going there; otherwise, you had to rely on photos and videos as your only window into the experience. Social interaction was limited to texts, phone calls, and video calls. But then came VR. With just a headset, you are no longer tied to a specific location or even to reality. You don't need to be in the same room as your friends to play together. You can meet in fully immersive virtual worlds where everything feels real. Want to explore new places? You can do it right from your couch. And when it comes to socialising, avatars take the place of physical presence.

VR breaks down the boundaries of space and possibility, offering a completely new way to experience and connect with the world.

At the same time, Mixed Reality (MR) and Augmented Reality (AR) both add digital elements to our world, but in different ways. AR overlays digital images, text, or animations onto the real world, but these elements don't interact with their surroundings. MR, on the other hand, merges the digital and physical worlds, allowing them to interact and respond to each other in real time. In MR, holograms aren't just static images - they're digital elements that interact with the real world, floating, blending, or even anchoring themselves into your environment. Imagine holograms walking across your floor, a digital pet that hides behind your real sofa, or a virtual to-do list you can pin to your actual fridge door. Unlike VR, where you're fully immersed in a digital landscape, MR keeps you grounded in the physical world, adding digital layers that enhance your reality, not replace it.[14]

The goal is simple. To make you feel like you're really there in the virtual worlds. Whether it's VR or MR, both revolve around one powerful concept called "presence". Even if it's artificial, presence tricks your brain into believing you are not just looking at a screen, you're inside the experience. And sometimes, that illusion is enough to make you feel a little less alone, even when you actually are.[15] These technologies create immersive spaces where people can connect and express themselves without making any adjustments to their daily routines. It offers a chance to be anywhere you want. With anyone you want. Across continents, time zones, and maybe even realities.

So, beyond all the impressive breakthroughs VR and MR bring to education, healthcare, design, and entertainment, there's this quiet, compelling hope attached to them–could they also help ease our loneliness? On paper, it sounds promising.

For those dealing with social anxiety or mental health issues, VR can be a game-changer. It offers a safe, controlled environment to practice conversations, build confidence, and engage with others without the pressure of face-to-face interaction. It's social training wheels with a reset button. Platforms like VRChat, AltspaceVR, and Rec Room give users the chance to hang out, play games, attend virtual concerts, or just casually chat through customisable avatars. These virtual hangouts can mimic real-life socialising dynamics, helping ease isolation and even spark meaningful relationships.[16]

In the Metaverse, you can create a fully customised avatar, hang out with friends, and dive into virtual experiences like concerts or art exhibits. By 2030, experts predict that over 1.4 billion people will be engaging with the Metaverse regularly, making it a major platform not only for entertainment but also for combating loneliness and building virtual communities.[17]

Companies like Sony, with the PSVR2, and Valve, with the Index, are racing to push the boundaries of realism in virtual worlds. And it's not just about sharper graphics or cooler gear–it's about creating spaces that feel real enough to matter. VR and MR aren't just emerging technologies; they're being sold as a cure for the quiet, growing ache of modern loneliness. It's a big leap forward, one that brings us closer to making virtual presence feel almost human.

But before we get too carried away with visions of a virtual utopia, it's worth stopping to ask: Are we really looking at a fairy tale solution here? If we're counting on the Metaverse, VR, or MR to fix all our feelings of loneliness and give us a happily-ever-after free from isolation, we might just be living in a digital bubble.

As appealing as it sounds, studies reveal something important: while virtual companionship can certainly help alleviate some forms of loneliness, it falls short when it comes to offering the depth and authenticity of real, face-to-face human connection. In other words, today's children might grow up feeling perfectly at ease sharing their deepest thoughts with digital companions in virtual worlds, treating them like trusted confidants. It's convenient, it's easy, and it's always there. But if that comfort comes at the cost of seeking real, human connection, we may be drifting into dangerous territory.

Sure, VR social platforms offer avatar-based interactions, but can they truly replicate the subtle, powerful language of human presence, eye contact, touch, the emotional nuance of a glance or a pause? MR tools, meanwhile, allow users to interact with digital content while still physically present with others. But doesn't that open the door to ignoring the very people standing right in front of us? As VR becomes more immersive and MR begins to overlay fantasy onto reality, we have to ask ourselves: Are we heading toward a "better-than-real-life" syndrome?

The illusion of connection might ease short-term loneliness, but over time, this gradual shift away from real interaction could lead us straight into the very isolation we're trying to escape. Whether it's gaming, socialising, exploring creativity, or living out power fantasies, activities in VR and MR are often designed to trigger the brain's reward system. Each interaction can trigger a hit of dopamine, delivering a quick rush of pleasure that keeps us coming back for more. This sets up a cycle of repeated use, similar to the mechanisms behind social media addiction. The more we dive into these alternate realities, the more we risk losing sight of what makes a real human connection so irreplaceable.

In virtual environments, we get to craft idealised versions of ourselves–avatars that are fitter, more confident, wealthier, even taller than we are in real life. At first, it feels empowering or a break from society's constant judgment. But over time, this digital perfection can quietly pull us away from our flaws, our emotional pain, our vulnerability.

Some users may become so reliant on VR and MR as a way to escape real-world issues that they start neglecting actual relationships and responsibilities. VR can simulate social presence, but it often falls short when it comes to replicating the emotional richness of real-world interactions, leaving users with a sense of emptiness after prolonged use.[18] What starts as an escape from loneliness may ultimately lead to deeper isolation, creating a paradox where the more we immerse ourselves in virtual connection, the further we drift from the fulfilling, imperfect human bonds that ground us.

If VR and MR are still being pitched as the next great antidote to loneliness without addressing the deeper consequences of relying on tech for human connection, then we can't ignore the bigger question: Who actually gets to access this solution?

While the technology is groundbreaking, it's also expensive, exclusive, and often inaccessible to many. A decent VR setup, including headsets and accessories can range anywhere from $500 to $5000. That's a huge investment, one that instantly puts this "cure" out of reach for millions. These high costs make VR and MR inaccessible to those in lower-income communities or less economically developed regions. We're talking about a world where nearly 2 billion people experience significant loneliness. Can we really assume that all of them will one day own high-end headsets and have access to the bandwidth, space, and support these systems require?

Loneliness doesn't just affect wealthy families. It affects people from every walk of life. So why are we tying the solution to something so exclusive? If VR and MR are meant to bring people together, shouldn't they be built for everyone, not just for those who can afford it?

Another concern that's raising eyebrows is this: Are we truly trying to solve the problem of loneliness through technology, or are we just creating a profitable industry out of human disconnection? The rise of AI-powered companions, VR, and MR promises emotional support, but behind the comforting voices and seamless interactions lies something more complex. Let's not forget that these digital companions are also programmed to manipulate emotions for profit. Aren't we noticing that our vulnerabilities, fears, and desires are being studied and exploited, as these platforms use the perfect combination of words, gestures, and responses to keep us hooked? Our moments of loneliness become data points. Our cravings for connection are optimised and monetised. So, as we turn to these technologies for connection, the real question is: are we becoming the product along the way?

Undoubtedly, the initial breakthroughs in AI, VR and MR seemed to create an environment where we are constantly surrounded by connections, virtually, at least. But as time passes, these platforms are slowly becoming a crutch we never knew we needed. The future of loneliness and connection in the age of AI, VR, and MR is a complex and evolving story. While it's still too early to say whether these technologies will solve loneliness or present challenges we haven't yet foreseen, one thing is crystal clear: no matter how advanced these virtual worlds become, they can never, I repeat, never, replace the beautifully imperfect, unpredictable, and deeply human need we have for one another.

Before VR and MR become second nature, we have to pause and ask ourselves: **Are we building a new kind of home–or are we quietly deepening the roots of loneliness?**

It's All About Setting Boundaries

"All of our technology is completely useless without the ability to have a conversation, to express feelings, to communicate."

– Sherry Turkle

Whether we like it or not, technology is where the world is headed, and it is moving fast. Yes, there's a lot of debate about the risks of AI and the rise of virtual experiences. And those debates need to happen. But at the same time, we can't ignore the fact that when someone is craving connection the most, it's often technology that shows up first. Not because it's the best option, but because it's the easiest one to reach.

So instead of pushing back against technology, maybe it's time we asked a better question: How can it work with our lives, not take them over?

A simple yet essential step in making technology truly serve us is learning to set boundaries. Whether it's an AI companion offering a comforting voice or a VR/MR experience pulling us into another world, it's important to set limits, both in time and emotional investment. Time boundaries on digital platforms protect us from slipping into excessive use that often leaves us feeling even more disconnected than before. It's easy to lose hours in the digital world, only to emerge feeling lonelier, not comforted. So, just like we block out time for work, rest, or a morning run, we owe it to ourselves to carve out moments for calls with family, spontaneous chats with a neighbour, even sitting in silence with a friend. It's not about rejecting technology; it's about not letting it replace what's irreplaceable.

Emotional boundaries, on the other hand, keep us grounded. It reminds us not to let surface-level interactions erode the depth of our real-life relationships. After spending time with a digital companion, ask yourself: *"Do I feel truly better, or just momentarily distracted?"* If what you're doing feels more like an escape than actual relief, that's your quiet reminder: human connection might be the missing piece.

Every time you dive into a virtual experience, make it a point to bring some of that magic into the real world. Just enjoyed a mixed reality concert? Awesome, but send a text to a friend and share the thrill of it with them. Spent time hanging out in a VR social space? Follow it up by setting up a board game night with your actual friends. Watched a movie with a friend's hologram? Plan to meet them for real, too. These virtual platforms can add something valuable to your life, but they shouldn't be an escape. Let them amplify your social world, not replace the interactions that truly matter. After all, technology is just a tool; its purpose is to enhance, not to disconnect.

With mindful use, technology can become a powerful tool for connection, particularly in supporting mental well-being. In the case of mental health issues, tech isn't just a convenience–it's a lifeline. But ultimately, boundaries that give us the power to use these platforms in a way that actually serves us. AI-based therapies and virtual mental health support groups can certainly provide accessible help, especially for those who might not otherwise have resources. But they should never stand alone. These technologies can be powerful tools, but they must be part of a broader support system that includes real human interaction and professional guidance. In short, technology should be a supplement to mental health care, not a replacement for the real, human touch that's essential to healing.

No matter how real AI, VR, or MR interactions might feel, they're still just simulations at the end of the day. While it's easy to point fingers at these technologies for collecting our personal data, our emotions, preferences, conversations, behaviours, the truth is that's how they're built. That's the function. It's on us to recognise when technology starts to cross emotional lines–and to draw clear ones in return.

Bots and virtual experiences might offer easy companionship or entertainment, but some are designed to feed emotional dependency. The more we lean on them for connection, the more we risk forgetting how to connect with actual people. That's where boundaries come in. Think of boundaries as guardrails that keep you from falling too deep into the endless scroll or getting lost in a digital illusion. Set those boundaries with care. Make them compassionate, both for yourself and the people around you. But above all, remember: you're the one in control. Use the technology, don't let it use you.

Machines have a gift for doing what they do best, such as automating tasks, processing data, and handling the kind of repetitive work that once drained our time and energy.In these areas, they excel. But when it comes to something more subtle, more human–like empathy, understanding, or emotional connection–that's where we, as humans, should have the upper hand.

Yes, machines can mimic empathy. They can offer comforting words or predict our needs. But machines can't truly replicate the depth of understanding and the genuine emotional exchange we humans crave. If we, as humans, ever fall short in this area, if we fail to connect with one another, then it's not an opportunity to introduce more technology. It's a failure in our own humanity. It's a reminder that we've lost something important along the way. In this case, it's time to rebuild what we've lost and reconnect with the very essence of what it means to be human.

Aristotle's concept of the Golden Mean teaches us that both excess and deficiency lead to vice, while true virtue lies in balance. It's not about swinging from one extreme to another, but about finding a middle ground that fosters long-term growth and fulfilment. In the context of combating loneliness, this principle is crucial. The answer is not to immerse ourselves excessively in technology, nor to reject it entirely. Instead, it's about cultivating a healthy balance between the digital and physical worlds.

As we navigate this new frontier of technology, we must remember that the ultimate goal isn't just connection for the sake of connection, but authentic connection. The one that feels as real and substantial as the people we share our lives with. These genuine bonds are what give life its true depth and meaning.

But the choice is ours: **Will we allow technology to amplify what's already there, or will we let it take us further away from the human experiences that matter most?** The path forward is ours to choose, and it's one that could ultimately shape whether loneliness becomes our fate or not.

ACKNOWLEDGMENT

This book is my first real attempt at creating the kind of change I want to see in the world. It is a slight push toward a more thoughtful and kinder society. If you are holding this book and reading these words, thank you. You made this possible just by being curious enough to pick it up.

What you are holding is the result of years of reading, researching, starting over, and writing draft after draft. I wouldn't have made it this far without the people who stood by me, kept me grounded, and reminded me why this mattered. I'm so deeply grateful to everyone who's been part of this journey.

To my father, Dr. Sarat Borkataki, who introduced me to books and the power of language. He gave me a way to explore the world and helped me see things from different angles. His encouragement still echoes in everything I write.

To my mother, Dipika Laskar, who believed in me even when I didn't. She's the one who kept pushing me to publish this book, who always stood in my corner, cheering me on. She taught me how to grow into myself, how to be at peace in my own company, and how to keep going when things got hard.

To my husband, Maninder Singh, who gave me the courage to leave behind a stable IT career to chase this dream. This book would still be an idea buried in my notes if not for him. No matter how messy or unpolished my drafts were, he read them all patiently and thoughtfully and helped me shape them into something real. Because of him, I get to dream big and know someone's got my back when it's time to get practical.

To my friends, who reminded me that honest, meaningful connections are still possible in a digital world that often feels rushed and superficial. They showed me that vulnerability isn't weakness, and real friendship can carry us through even our loneliest seasons.

Finally, to Clever Fox Publishing, who gave me this platform and helped turn a dream into something tangible. Thank you for believing in this book and in me.

SOURCES

Introduction

1. SEO.AI, "Social Media Users Worldwide 2024"
2. U.S. Department of Health and Human Services. (2023). *Our Epidemic of Loneliness and Isolation.*
3. International Institute for Population Sciences (IIPS) & Ministry of Health and Family Welfare. (2020). *Longitudinal Ageing Study in India (LASI), Wave 1, 2017–18, National Report.*
4. Jo Cox Commission on Loneliness. (2017). *Combatting Loneliness One Conversation at a Time.*
5. Japan Today. (2024, December 25). *39% of people living in Japan feel lonely: Gov't study.*
6. Business Standard. (2024, October 24). *Lonely deaths rise in South Korea: Can a $327 mn plan end the isolation?*
7. Alberti, F. B. (2019). A biography of loneliness: The history of an emotion. Oxford University Press.
8. Thoreau, H. D. (1854). Walden; or, life in the woods, Bobonich, C. (2019). *Aristotle's ethics.* In E. N. Zalta (Ed.), *The Stanford Encyclopedia of Philosophy* (Fall 2019 Edition). Cohen, J. (2020). *Rousseau.* In E. N. Zalta (Ed.), *The Stanford Encyclopedia of Philosophy* (Fall 2020 Edition).

9. Newport Institute. (2024). *Loneliness and depression in young adults.*
10. Burrell, M. (2023, November 16). *'As bad as 15 cigarettes a day': WHO declares loneliness a global health concern. London Evening Standard.*

Choice 1

1. Festinger, L. (1957). A theory of cognitive dissonance.
2. Parr, B. (2015). Captivology: The science of capturing people's attention. HarperOne.
3. DemandSage. (2025). *32 creator economy statistics 2025: Market size data.* https://www.demandsage.com/creator-economy-statistics/
4. Abbott, B., & Krasner, J. (1982). Berenice Abbott: A Life in Photography. New York Graphic Society.
5. Gilovich, T., Medvec, V. H., & Savitsky, K. (2000). The spotlight effect in social judgment: An egocentric bias in estimates of the salience of one's own actions and appearance. Journal of Personality and Social Psychology, 78(2), 211–222.
6. Maslow, A. H. (1943). A theory of human motivation. Psychological Review, 50(4), 370–396.
7. Gardner, W. L., Pickett, C. L., & Knowles, M. (2005). Social snacking and shielding: Using social symbols, selves, and surrogates in the service of belonging needs. In K. D. Williams, J. P. Forgas, & W. von Hippel (Eds.), *The social*

outcast: Ostracism, social exclusion, rejection, and bullying (pp. 227–241). New York: Psychology Press.

8. Less in-person social interaction with peers among U.S. adolescents in the 2010s and links to loneliness.Journal of Social and Personal Relationships, 38(6), 1723–1744
9. Kontras, A. (2000). *The Journey.*
10. Business Insider India. (2022). *Multiple revenue streams powering India's digital creators.* Business Insider India.
11. Horton, D., & Wohl, R. R. (1956). Mass communication and para-social interaction: Observations on intimacy at a distance. *Psychiatry,* 19(3), 215–229.
12. Barker, V. (2018). Performing the Self Online: Social Media and Identity Construction. Journal of Digital Culture, 12(3), 45–60, Marwick, A. E. (2013). Status Update: Celebrity, Publicity, and Branding in the Social Media Age. Yale University Press.
13. Hammersley, B. (2004, February 12). Podcasting: Audio on the internet comes of age. *The Guardian,* Stark, L. (2019). Podcasting: New Aural Cultures and Digital Media. Palgrave Macmillan, McHugh, S. (2016). How podcasting is changing the audio storytelling genre. *The Radio Journal: International Studies in Broadcast & Audio Media,* 14(1), 65–82
14. Descript. (2025). The history of podcasts: From RSS beginnings to 2025.
15. Banjoko, I. (2023, May 30). 2023 Podcast market valued at USD 23.63b – Report. *Marketing Edge Magazine,* Grand View Research. (2025). *Podcasting market size and share | Industry report, 2030.*

16. Horton, D., & Wohl, R. R. (1956). Mass communication and parasocial interaction: Observations on intimacy at a distance. *Psychiatry*, 19(3), 215–229.
17. World Economic Forum. (2022, September 6). The rise of the creator economy: How entrepreneurs are thriving in a new era.
18. Misra, S., Cheng, L., Genevie, J., & Yuan, M. (2016). "The iPhone Effect: The Quality of In-Person Social Interactions in the Presence of Mobile Devices." *Environment and Behavior, 48*(2), 275-298, Przybylski, A. K., & Weinstein, N. (2013). Can you connect with me now? How the presence of mobile communication technology influences face-to-face conversation quality. *Environment and Behavior*, 45(3), 285–298.
19. Pariser, E. (2011). The filter bubble: What the Internet is hiding from you. Penguin Press.
20. Schultz, W. (2016). Dopamine reward prediction-error signalling: A two-component response. *Nature Reviews Neuroscience, 17*(3), 183–195, Montag, C., Alter, A. (2017). Irresistible: The rise of addictive technology and the business of keeping us hooked. Penguin Press.

Choice 2

1. The Indian Express. (2023). *Facing derogatory slurs and stereotypes: The Northeast's struggle against discrimination.*
2. Office of the Registrar General & Census Commissioner, India, Ministry of Home Affairs, Government of India. (2020). *Official Languages of India.*

3. Hu, X., Zhang, L., & Liu, X. (2024). Lower class competence stereotypes of the upper class increase class conflict: The mediating role of intergroup envy and the moderating role of upward social mobility belief. *Frontiers in Psychology*, 15, 1360951, Fiske, S. T., Cuddy, A. J. C., & Glick, P. (2007). Universal dimensions of social perception: Warmth and competence. *Trends in Cognitive Sciences*, 11(2), 77–83.
4. Aristotle. (trans. 1991). *Politics* (T. A. Sinclair, Trans.). Penguin Classics, Baumeister, R. F., & Leary, M. R. (1995). The need to belong: Desire for interpersonal attachments as a fundamental human motivation. *Psychological Bulletin*, 117(3), 497–529.
5. Hall, E. (2010). Greek Tragedy: Suffering under the Sun. Oxford University Press, Jung, C. G. (1953). *Two Essays on Analytical Psychology* (R. F. C. Hull, Trans.). Princeton University Press. (Original work published 1928), Machiavelli, N. (2003). *The Prince* (H. C. Mansfield, Trans.). University of Chicago Press. (Original work published 1532)
6. Briggs, A. (1990). Victorian People: A Reassessment of Persons and Themes, 1851-67. University of Chicago Press.
7. Smith-Rosenberg, C. (1985). Disorderly Conduct: Visions of Gender in Victorian America. Oxford University Press
8. The Economic Times. (2019). *Marriage accounts for 20% of all loans among young Indians: Survey*. Referencing the IndiaLends survey.
9. Kim, S. (2019). The Social Significance of Weddings in South Korea: Status, Tradition, and Modernity. Journal of Korean Studies, 24(2), 105–128

10. Coontz, S. (2006). The Wedding Complex: How the Wedding Industry Shapes Expectations and Costs. In Marriage, a History: How Love Conquered Marriage (pp. 123–147). Penguin Books.
11. Ridgeway, C. L. (2011). Framed by Gender: How Gender Inequality Persists in the Modern World. Oxford University Press.
12. Banerjee, A. V. (1992). A simple model of herd behavior. *The Quarterly Journal of Economics*, 107(3), 797–817
13. Rogers, C. R. (1959). A theory of therapy, personality, and interpersonal relationships: As developed in the client-centered framework. In S. Koch (Ed.), *Psychology: A study of a science* (Vol. 3, pp. 184–256). McGraw-Hill.
14. Izuma, K., Saito, D. N., & Sadato, N. (2008). Processing of social and monetary rewards in the human striatum. *Neuron*, 58(2), 284-294, Kringelbach, M. L., & Berridge, K. C. (2009). Towards a functional neuroanatomy of pleasure and happiness. *Trends in Cognitive Sciences*, 13(11), 479-487, Andrews-Hanna, J. R., Smallwood, J., & Spreng, R. N. (2014). The default network and self-generated thought: component processes, dynamic control, and clinical relevance. *Annals of the New York Academy of Sciences*, 1316(1), 29-52, Yeshurun, Y., Nguyen, M., & Hasson, U. (2021). The default mode network: where the idiosyncratic self meets the shared social world. *Nature Reviews Neuroscience*, 22(3), 181-192.
15. Mathew, T. (2011). Ratan Tata: The Authorized Biography. HarperCollins India.

16. Remnick, D. (2010). The Bridge: The Life and Rise of Barack Obama. Knopf.
17. Brown, B. (2012). Daring Greatly: How the Courage to Be Vulnerable Transforms the Way We Live, Love, Parent, and Lead. Gotham Books
18. Basu, K. (2011, May 26). Tagore and his India. *The New York Review of Books,* Tagore, R. (1961). *Towards universal man.* Asia Publishing House, Sen, A. (2005). The argumentative Indian: Writings on Indian history, culture and identity. Farrar, Straus and Giroux.
19. Goleman, D. (1995). Emotional intelligence: Why it can matter more than IQ. Bantam Books.
20. National Commission for Protection of Child Rights (NCPCR). (2021). *Bullying in schools: A study of prevalence and impact.* New Delhi: NCPCR, McAfee. (2021). *Cyberbullying in plain sight: A global study.*
21. Russell, A. E., Ford, T., Williams, R., & Russell, G. (2019). The association between bullying and adolescent self-harm: A systematic review and meta-analysis. *The Lancet Psychiatry, 6*(1), 48–58.

Choice 3

1. Goleman, D. (1995). Emotional intelligence: Why it can matter more than IQ. Bantam Books.
2. Rizzolatti, G., & Craighero, L. (2004). The mirror-neuron system. *Annual Review of Neuroscience*, 27, 169-192.

3. Keysers, C., & Gazzola, V. (2009). Expanding the mirror: vicarious activity for actions, emotions, and sensations. *Current Opinion in Neurobiology*, 19(6), 666–671.
4. Decety, J., & Jackson, P. L. (2004). The functional architecture of human empathy. *Behavioral and Cognitive Neuroscience Reviews*, 3(2), 71–100.
5. Batson, C. D. (2011). *Altruism in humans*. Oxford University Press.
6. Putnam, R. D. (2000). Bowling alone: The collapse and revival of American community. Simon & Schuster.
7. Konrath, S. H., O'Brien, E., & Hsing, C. (2011). Changes in dispositional empathy in American college students over time: A meta-analysis. *Personality and Social Psychology Review, 15*(2), 180–198.
8. Gallup (2022). "State of the Global Workplace: The Voice of the World's Employees."
9. Hoffman, M. L. (2000). Empathy and Moral Development: Implications for Caring and Justice. Cambridge University Press.
10. Bowlby, J. (1969). Attachment and Loss: Vol. 1. Attachment.
11. Gottman, J. M., & Silver, N. (1999). The Seven Principles for Making Marriage Work. Crown Publishing Group.
12. Singer, T., et al. (2004). Empathy for pain involves the affective but not sensory components of pain. Science, 303(5661), 1157–1162, Roy, M., Shohamy, D., & Wager, T. D. (2012). Ventromedial prefrontal-subcortical systems and the generation of affective meaning. Trends in Cognitive Sciences, 16(3), 147–156, Morelli, S. A., Sacchet, M. D., & Zaki, J. (2015). Common and distinct neural

correlates of personal and vicarious reward: A quantitative meta-analysis. NeuroImage, 112, 244–253, Eisenberger, N. I. (2012). The neural bases of social pain: Evidence for shared representations with physical pain. Nature Reviews Neuroscience, 13(6), 421–434, Inagaki, T. K., & Eisenberger, N. I. (2016). Giving support to others reduces sympathetic nervous system-related responses to stress. Psychophysiology, 53(4), 427–435.

13. Heinrichs, M., Baumgartner, T., Kirschbaum, C., & Ehlert, U. (2003).Social support and oxytocin interact to suppress cortisol and subjective responses to psychosocial stress. Biological Psychiatry, 54(12), 1389–1398.
14. Goleman, D. (1995). Emotional Intelligence: Why It Can Matter More Than IQ. New York: Bantam Books, Singer, T., Seymour, B., O'Doherty, J., Kaube, H., Dolan, R. J., & Frith, C. D. (2004). *Empathy for pain involves the affective but not sensory components of pain. Science*, 303(5661), 1157–1162.
15. Decety, J., & Yoder, K. J. (2017). Empathy and motivation for helping: Cognitive empathy, emotional empathy, and altruistic motivation. Current Opinion in Psychology, 19, 73–77, Batson, C. D. (2011). *Altruism in Humans.* Oxford University Press.
16. Brown, B. (2010). The gifts of imperfection: Let go of who you think you're supposed to be and embrace who you are. Hazelden Publishing.
17. Davis, M. H. (2018). Empathy: A social psychological approach (2nd ed.). Routledge.

18. Kidd, D. C., & Castano, E. (2013). Reading literary fiction improves theory of mind. *Science*, 342(6156), 377–380

Choice 4

1. Snyder, Gary. *The Practice of the Wild.* San Francisco: North Point Press, 1990.
2. IQAir. (2024). World Air Quality Report 2023.
3. National Parks Board Singapore. (n.d.). *City in Nature,* Gardens by the Bay. (n.d.). *About the Supertree Grove,* World Economic Forum. (2018). *How Singapore is creating a green, liveable city.*
4. World Bank. (n.d.). *Costa Rica: Overview.*
5. Lee, J. H., & Anderson, C. K. (2013). *The Cheonggyecheon Restoration Project: A Case Study of Urban Renewal in Seoul, South Korea.* International Journal of Environmental Studies, 70(3), 348–363.
6. Wikipedia contributors. (2024, June 20). *Leisure Valley, Chandigarh.* Wikipedia, Chandigarh Administration. (n.d.). *The Edict of Chandigarh.*
7. Eck, D. L. (2013). India: A sacred geography. Harmony Books.
8. Kraut, R. (2018). *Aristotle: Political philosophy.* In E. N. Zalta (Ed.), *The Stanford Encyclopedia of Philosophy* (Fall 2018 Edition).
9. Basu, A., & Katti, M. (2019). Spending time in nature reduces cortisol levels and promotes well-being: Evidence

from a systematic review and meta-analysis. *Frontiers in Psychology, 10*, Article 274.

10. University of East Anglia. (2018). Exposure to green space linked to reduced physiological stress markers: A systematic review of over 140 studies. *Nature Communications.*
11. Soga, M., Gaston, K. J., & Yamaura, Y. (2021). A global meta-analysis on the link between natural environments and loneliness. *Scientific Reports, 11*(1), 10091.
12. Kaplan, S. (1995). The restorative benefits of nature: Toward an integrative framework. *Journal of Environmental Psychology*, 15(3), 169–182.
13. Li, Q. (2018). Forest bathing: How trees can help you find health and happiness. Viking.
14. Selhub, E. M., & Logan, A. C. (2012). Your Brain on Nature: The Science of Nature's Influence on Your Health, Happiness and Vitality. Wiley.
15. Kahn, P. H., & Kellert, S. R. (Eds.). (2002). Children and Nature: Psychological, Sociocultural, and Evolutionary Investigations. MIT Press.
16. Wilson, E. O. (1984). *Biophilia*. Harvard University Press.
17. Lambert, G. W., Reid, C., Kaye, D. M., Jennings, G. L., & Esler, M. D. (2002). Effect of sunlight and season on serotonin turnover in the brain. *The Lancet*, 360(9348), 1840-1842.
18. Wilson, R. (2016). *John Muir: Nature's Visionary*. National Geographic Society.
19. Worster, D. (2008). A Passion for Nature: The Life of John Muir. Oxford University Press.
20. Thoreau, H. D. (1854). Walden; or, Life in the Woods.

21. Times of India. (2023, June 15). *Understanding Generation Beta: Future of 2.1 billion lives shaped by technology and climate*. Times of India.
22. Cabinet OKs green law for eco-friendly ULBs. (2025, June 21). *Times of India*.
23. White, M. P., Alcock, I., Grellier, J., Wheeler, B. W., Hartig, T., Warber, S. L., Bone, A., Depledge, M. H., & Fleming, L. E. (2019). Spending at least 120 minutes a week in nature is associated with good health and well-being. *Scientific Reports, 9*(1), 7730

Choice 5

1. Newport, C. (2019). Digital minimalism: Choosing a focused life in a noisy world. Portfolio.
2. MindGenic AI Project. (2023, December 12). *Research: 65% of Gen Z experience loneliness regularly. Science in Poland.*
3. Koch, C. (2018). The joy of solitude: A guide to embracing alone time and finding peace within. HarperOne.
4. Long, C. R., & Averill, J. R. (2003). Solitude: An exploration of benefits of being alone. *Journal for the Theory of Social Behaviour*, *33*(1), 21–44, Cacioppo, J. T., & Cacioppo, S. (2018). Loneliness in the modern age: An evolutionary theory of loneliness (ETL). *Advances in Experimental Social Psychology*, *58*, 127–197.
5. Andrews-Hanna, J. R., Smallwood, J., & Spreng, R. N. (2014). The default network and self-generated thought:

Component processes, dynamic control, and clinical relevance. *Annals of the New York Academy of Sciences, 1316*(1), 29–52.

6. Tang, Y.-Y., Hölzel, B. K., & Posner, M. I. (2015). The neuroscience of mindfulness meditation. *Nature Reviews Neuroscience, 16*(4), 213–225.
7. Isaacson, W. (2011). *Steve Jobs.* New York, NY: Simon & Schuster.
8. Rubin, J. (2014). Haruki Murakami and the music of words. Columbia University Press.
9. Rolland, R. (1957). *The life of Vivekananda and the universal gospel* (M. Prabhavananda, Trans.). Vedanta Press. (Original work published 1929)
10. Rilke, R. M. (1934). *Letters to a young poet* (M. D. Herter Norton, Trans.). W. W. Norton & Company. (Original work published 1929)
11. Isaacson, W. (2007). Einstein: His life and universe. Simon & Schuster.
12. Flood, G. (1996). *An introduction to Hinduism.* Cambridge University Press.
13. Easwaran, E. (2007). *The Upanishads* (2nd ed.). Nilgiri Press.
14. *Bhagavad Gita* 6.10, translated by A.C. Bhaktivedanta Swami Prabhupada
15. Ñāṇananda, K. (2014). *Nibbāna - The Mind Stilled* (Vol. 1). Buddhist Publication Society, Bodhi, B. (Trans.). (2000). The connected discourses of the Buddha: A new translation of the Saṃyutta Nikāya. Wisdom Publications.

16. Suzuki, D. T. (1956). Zen Buddhism and Japanese Culture. Princeton University Press, Juniper, A. (2003). Wabi Sabi: The Japanese Art of Impermanence. Tuttle Publishing, Li, Q. (2018). Forest Bathing: How Trees Can Help You Find Health and Happiness. Viking.
17. Buswell, R. E. (1992). The Zen Monastic Experience: Buddhist Practice in Contemporary Korea. Princeton University Press., Kim, E. (2021). Honjok: The Art of Living Alone in Korea. Penguin Books, Kim, S., & Park, Y. (2020). Solitary living and its cultural reinterpretation in South Korea: The rise of Honjok. *Journal of Contemporary Korean Studies*, 7(1), 45–62.
18. Yun, S. (1651/2005). The Fisherman's Calendar (translated by Peter H. Lee). In Lee, P. H. (Ed.), Anthology of Korean Literature: From Early Times to the Nineteenth Century (pp. 184–188). University of Hawaii Press.
19. Gelter, H. (2000). Friluftsliv: The Scandinavian philosophy of outdoor life. Canadian Journal of Environmental Education, 5(1), 77–92, Wiking, M. (2017). The little book of hygge: The Danish way to live well. Penguin Life.
20. LeDoux, J. (2015). Anxious: Using the brain to understand and treat fear and anxiety. Viking.
21. Brown, B. (2010). The gifts of imperfection: Let go of who you think you're supposed to be and embrace who you are. Hazelden Publishing.
22. Storr, A. (1988). Solitude: A return to the self. Free Press.

Choice 6

1. Bradshaw, T. (2025, February 7). Big Tech lines up over $300bn in AI spending for 2025. Financial Times.
2. Kuyda, E. (2024, August 12). *Replika CEO Eugenia Kuyda says it's okay if we end up marrying AI chatbots*. The Verge.
3. Fitzpatrick, K. K., Darcy, A., & Vierhile, M. (2017). Delivering cognitive behavior therapy to young adults with symptoms of depression and anxiety using a fully automated conversational agent (Woebot): A randomized controlled trial. JMIR Mental Health, 4(2), e19.
4. Aggarwal, J., & Vempati, R. (2023, October 10). *Wysa: Transforming mental health through AI-driven support*. EMHIC Global.
5. GROOVE X. (2018, December 18). *GROOVE X introduces a new companion robot, 'LOVOT'*. PR Newswire.
6. Ghafurian, M., Ellard, C., & Dautenhahn, K. (2020). Social companion robots to reduce isolation: A perception change due to COVID-19.
7. Wang, W., & Toscano, M. (2024). *Artificial Intelligence and Relationships: 1 in 4 Young Adults Believe AI Partners Could Replace Real-life Romance*. Institute for Family Studies.
8. Meta Platforms, Inc. (2022, October 11). Meta will integrate Zoom and Microsoft Teams into its VR workspaces. *Yahoo Finance*.
9. Microsoft. (2024, January 24). *Bring virtual connections to life with Microsoft Mesh now generally available in Microsoft Teams*. Microsoft 365 Blog.
10. Apple Inc. (2024, January 8). *Apple Vision Pro available in the U.S. on February 2*. Apple Newsroom.

11. Lyons-Cunha, J. (2024, December 19). *What are AI companions?* Built In.
12. Kalra, Y. (2024, December 10). Satya Nadella's vision for Microsoft: AI, AI and AI. *BankInfoSecurity*.
13. Harari, Y. N. (2018). 21 Lessons for the 21st Century (pp. 112–115).
14. Weaver, J. (2025, May 28). *Mixed Reality vs. Augmented Reality: What's the difference and why does it matter?* Nextech AR Solutions. Microsoft. (n.d.). What is mixed reality?
15. Slater, M., & Sanchez-Vives, M. V. (2016). Enhancing our lives with immersive virtual reality. *Frontiers in Robotics and AI*, 3, 74.
16. Freeman, D., Haselton, P., Freeman, J., Spanlang, B., Kishore, S., Albery, E., ... & Slater, M. (2018). Automated psychological therapy using immersive virtual reality for treatment of fear of heights: A single-blind, parallel-group, randomised controlled trial. *The Lancet Psychiatry, 5*(8), 625–632, Kaimara, P., Ozoliņa-Ozola, I., & Dagdilelis, V. (2021). Virtual reality in education: A tool for social and emotional learning. *Education Sciences, 11*(4), 191, Wiederhold, B. K., & Riva, G. (2019). Virtual reality therapy: Emerging topics and future challenges. *Cyberpsychology, Behavior, and Social Networking, 22*(1), 3–6, Oh, C. S., Bailenson, J. N., & Welch, G. F. (2018). A systematic review of social presence: Definition, antecedents, and implications. *Frontiers in Robotics and AI, 5*, 114.
17. Analytics Insight. (2023, June 20). *1.4 billion users expected to join the metaverse by 2030*. Analytics Insight.

18. Riches, S., Vasalou, A., King, S., Carr, L., & Young, R. (2019). Social presence and emotional responses in virtual reality: A qualitative study of users' experiences. *International Journal of Human-Computer Studies, 126*, 1–12.